T0078236

RYSZARD KAPUŚCIŃSKI

Shah of Shahs

Ryszard Kapuściński was born in 1932. During four decades reporting on Asia, Latin America, and Africa, he befriended Che Guevara, Salvador Allende, and Patrice Lumumba. He witnessed twenty-seven coups and revolutions and was sentenced to death four times. His books have been translated into nineteen languages. He died in 2007.

INTERNATIONAL

Books by Ryszard Kapuściński

RYSZARD KAPUŚCIŃSKI

Shah of Shahs

*Translated from the Polish by
William R. Brand and
Katarzyna Mroczkowska-Brand*

*Vintage International
Vintage Books
A Division of Random House, Inc.
New York*

Library of Congress Cataloging-in-Publication Data
Kapuściński, Ryszard.
Shah of shahs.
Translation of Szachinszach.
Reprint. Originally published: San Diego:
Harcourt Brace Jovanovich © 1985.
1. Iran—Politics and government—1941-1979.
I. Title.
DS318.K31513   1986   955′.053   91-50497
ISBN 978-0-679-73801-5

CARDS, FACES,
FIELDS OF FLOWERS

Everything is in confusion, as though the police have just finished a violent, nervous search. Newspapers, local and foreign, are scattered everywhere, special editions, big attention-getting headlines,

He Has Left

large photos of a gaunt, elongated face, its controlled features so bent on showing neither anxiety nor defeat that it no longer expresses anything at all. Copies of later editions proclaim in fervor and triumph:

He Has Returned

A severe patriarchal face that has no intention of expressing anything at all fills the rest of the page.

(And between that departure and that return, what heights of emotion and fervor, rage and terror, how many conflagrations!)

On the floor, chairs, table, desk lie heaps of index cards, scraps of paper, notes so hastily scrawled and chaotic, I have to stop and think where I jotted down the sentence "He will deceive you and make promises to you, but don't let yourself be fooled." Who said that? When? To whom?

Or, covering a whole sheet of paper in red pencil:

"Must call 64-12-18." But so much time has passed, I can't remember whose number it is or why it was so important to call.

Unfinished letter, never mailed. I could go on at length about what I've seen and lived through here, but it is difficult to organize my impressions. . . .

The worst chaos is on the big round table: photos of various sizes, cassettes, 8-mm film, newsletters, photocopies of leaflets—all piled, mixed up together, helter-skelter, like a flea market. And more posters and albums, records and books acquired or given by people, the collected remnants of an era just ended but still able to be seen and heard because it has been preserved here on film—flowing, agitated rivers of people; on cassettes—the wail of the muezzins, shouted orders, conversations, monologues; in photos—faces in ecstasy, exaltation.

Now, at the very thought of trying to put everything in order (because the day I'm to leave is approaching), I am overcome by both aversion and profound fatigue. When I stay in a hotel (which is quite often) I like the room to be a mess because then the ambience has the illusion of some kind of life, a substitute warmth and intimacy, a proof (though illusory) that such a strange uncozy place, as all hotel rooms in essence are, has been at least partially conquered and tamed. In a room arranged into antiseptic order, I feel numb and lonely, pinched by all the straight lines, corners of furniture, flat walls, all that indifferent, stiff geometry, a strained, meticulous arrangement existing only for its own sake, without a trace of human presence. Fortunately, within a few hours of my arrival, influenced by my unconscious actions (the result of haste or laziness), the existing order breaks down, disappears, objects come to life,

4

begin moving from place to place, and enter into ever changing configurations and connections; things take on a cramped, baroque look, and, all at once, the room's atmosphere becomes friendlier and more familiar. Then I can take a deep breath and relax.

Right now I cannot summon up enough strength to do anything with the room, so I go downstairs, where four young men are drinking tea and playing cards in a gloomy, empty hall. They've abandoned themselves to some intricate game—neither bridge nor poker, black-jack nor pinochle—whose rules I'll probably never grasp. They use two sets of cards at once, playing in silence, until at a certain moment one of them takes all the cards, a delighted expression on his face. After a pause they deal, lay dozens of cards on the table, ponder, count, and begin quarreling as they count.

These four, the reception staff, live off me. I am supporting them because I am the only guest in the hotel. I also support the cleaning woman, cooks, waiters, launderers, janitors, gardener, and for all I know several other people and their families, too. I don't mean to say that if I delayed settling my bill they would all starve, but I try to keep my account paid just in case. Only a few months ago it was an achievement, like winning a lottery, to get a room in this city. Despite the many many hotels, there was such an avalanche of people that new arrivals had to rent beds in private hospitals just to have a place to stay. Now the boom of easy money and daz-zling transactions is over, the local businessmen are lying low, and the foreign partners have fled, leaving every-thing behind. Tourism has fallen to zero; all interna-tional traffic has frozen. Some hotels were burned down, others are closed or empty, and in one of them, guerril-las have set up their headquarters. Today the city is engrossed in its own affairs, it doesn't need foreigners, it doesn't need the world.

The cardplayers take a break from their game to offer me tea. Here they drink only tea or yogurt, not coffee or alcohol. For drinking alcohol you can get forty or even sixty lashes, and if someone brawny does the whipping (that type is often the most enthusiastic flogger) your back will be pulp. So we slurp our tea and watch the TV below the window at the other end of the hall.

Khomeini's face appears on the screen.

Khomeini is seated in a simple wooden armchair on a simple wooden platform in one of the squares of (to judge from the shabbiness of the buildings) a poor section of Qom. A small, flat, gray, charmless city, Qom lies a hundred miles south of Teheran in a vacant, wearying, parched, sunbaked desert. Nothing in that murderous climate would seem to favor reflection and contemplation, yet Qom is a place of religious fervor, rabid orthodoxy, mysticism, and faith militant. It contains five hundred mosques and the nation's biggest seminaries. Koranic scholars and the guardians of tradition quarrel in Qom; the venerable ayatollahs convene their councils there; Khomeini rules the country from Qom. He never leaves, never goes to the capital, never goes anywhere. He neither sightsees nor pays visits. He used to live with his wife and five children in Qom in a small house on a cramped, dusty, unpaved little street with a gutter running down the middle. Now he's moved to his daughter's house, from whose balcony he appears to the crowds in the street below (usually, zealous pilgrims visiting the mosques of the holy city and, most important of all, the tomb, forbidden to non-Muslims, of the Immaculate Fatima, sister of the eighth Imam Reza). Khomeini leads an ascetic life, eating only rice, yogurt, and fruit, and occupying but one room, bare walls, no furniture, only a bedroll on the floor, and a pile of books. Here, sitting on a blanket spread on the floor, leaning back against the wall, he receives his guests, including the most formal official foreign delegations. From the window he can see the domes of the mosques and the spacious courtyard of the medresh—an enclosed world of turquoise mosaics, bluish-green minarets, coolness and shade. All day a steady stream of guests and petitioners passes through this room. When there is a break, Khomeini goes off to pray or stays in his room, devoting the time to reflection or simply—as is natural for a man of eighty—taking a nap. The one with the most access to him is his younger son Ahmed, like his father a cleric. The other son, the first-born and the hope of his father's life, perished in mysterious circumstances— treacherously killed, people say, by Savak, the Shah's secret police.

The camera shows the square packed with people standing shoulder to shoulder. It shows curious and solemn faces. Off to the side, separated from the men in a clearly marked enclosure, stand women wrapped in chadors. It's a gray cloudy day, the crowd is charcoal-colored and, where the women stand, black. As always, Khomeini is dressed in loose-fitting dark clothes, a black turban on his head. He sits stiffly. His face is pale and still above his white beard. He does not gesticulate when he speaks; his hands rest on the arms of the chair. Once in a while he wrinkles his high forehead and raises his eyebrows; otherwise, not a muscle moves in the face of this man of immense stubborn, unretreating, unhesitating, implacable will. In this face, which seems to have been composed once and for all, yielding to neither emotions nor moods, expressing nothing but taut attentiveness and internal concentration, only the eyes move constantly. Their lively, incisive glance slides over the sea of curly heads, measures the depth of the square and the distance to its limits and continues its meticulous inspection as if insistently searching for a specific person. I listen to his monotonous voice, with its measured slow rhythm—a strong voice, but a voice that never leaps or flies, never betrays a mood, never sparkles.

"What is he talking about?" I ask the cardplayers, when Khomeini pauses for a moment to consider his next sentence.

"He is saying that we must preserve our dignity," one of them answers.

The cameraman pans across the roofs of the nearby houses where young people, with checkered scarves wrapped around their heads, stand, holding automatic rifles.

"And now what is he saying?" I ask again, because I don't understand Farsi.

"He is saying," one of the young men tells me, "in our country there is no room for foreign influence."

Khomeini goes on speaking and everyone follows attentively. On the screen someone's trying to quiet a group of children at the base of the platform.

"What is he saying?" I ask again after a while.

"He is saying that nobody will tell us what to do in our own home or impose anything on us, and he is saying: 'Be brothers to one another, be united.' "

That is all they can tell me in their halting English. Everyone learning English should understand that it is getting harder and harder to communicate in that language around the world. The same is true of French and, generally, of all European languages. Once Europe ruled the world, sending its merchants, soldiers, and missionaries to every continent, imposing on others its own interests and culture (this in usually rather bogus versions). Even in the remotest corners of the world, knowing a European language was a mark of distinction, testifying to an ambitious upbringing, and was often a necessity of life, the basis for career and promotion, and sometimes even a condition for being considered human. Those languages were taught in African schools, used in commerce, spoken in exotic parliaments, Asian courts, and Arab coffeehouses. Traveling almost anywhere in the world, Europeans could feel at home. They could express their opinions and understand what others were saying to them. Today the world is different. Hundreds of patriotisms have blossomed. Every nation wants to control and organize its own population, territory, resources, and culture according to native traditions. Every nation thinks it is or wants to be free, independent, cherishes its own values, and insists upon (and is particularly sensitive about getting) respect for them. Even small and weak nations—these especially—hate to be preached to, and rebel against anyone who tries to rule them or force often suspect values on them. People may admire the strength of others—but preferably at a safe remove and certainly not when used against them. Every power has its own dynamics, its own domineering, expansionist tendencies, its bullying obsessive need to trample the weak. This is the law of power, as everyone knows. But what can the weaker ones do? They can only fence themselves off, afraid of being swallowed up, stripped, regimented into a conformity of gait, face, expression, tongue, thought, response, ordered to give their life's blood for an alien cause, and of finally being crushed altogether. Hence their dissent and revolt, their struggle for independent existence, their struggle for their own language. In Syria the French newspaper was closed down; in Vietnam after the Americans left, the English-language paper, and now in Iran both French and English ones. On radio and television and during press conferences, only Farsi, their own language, is used. A man who can't read the Farsi sign on a woman's clothing store in Teheran—"Entry to this store by men is forbidden under penalty of arrest"—will go to jail. Someone else who cannot read the inscription near Isfahan that warns "Keep Out—Mines!" may die.

I used to carry a small transistor radio and listen to the local stations. No matter which continent I was on, I could always find out what was happening in the world. Now that radio is worthless. When I turn the dial I get ten stations, each using a different language, and I can't understand a word. If I travel a thousand miles, I get ten new equally incomprehensible stations. Are they saying that the money in my pocket is no longer any good? Are they saying that war has broken out?

Television is the same.

All over the world, at any hour, on a million screens an infinite number of people are saying something to us, trying to convince us of something, gesturing, making faces, getting excited, smiling, nodding their heads, pointing their fingers, and we don't know what it's about, what they want from us, what they are summoning us to. They might as well have come from a distant planet—an enormous army of public relations experts from Venus or Mars—yet they are our kin, with the same bones and blood as ours, with lips that move and audible voices, but we cannot understand a word. In what language will the universal dialogue of humanity be carried out? Several hundred languages are fighting for recognition and promotion; the language barriers are rising. Deafness and incomprehension are multiplying.

After a short break (during which they show fields of flowers—they love flowers here and plant colorful, luxuriant gardens around the tombs of their greatest poets) the photo of a young man appears on the screen. An announcer says something.

"What's he saying?" I ask my cardplayers.

"He's giving the name of the man in the photo. And telling who he was."

Then another photograph appears, and another—photos from student identity cards, framed pictures, snapshots from automatic photo machines, photographs with ruins in the background, one family portrait with an arrow pointing to a barely visible girl to show who is being described. Each photograph appears for a few moments; the list of names the announcer is reading goes on and on.

The parents are asking for information. They have been doing this for months, hoping against hope. The people in the photographs disappeared in September, December, January, that is, in the months of heaviest fighting, when the glow of fires over the city never died. They must have marched in the front ranks of the demonstration, right into the machine-gun fire. Or sharpshooters on nearby rooftops picked them off. We can suppose that each of these faces was last seen in the gun-sight of a soldier taking aim. Every evening, during this program, we listen to the announcer's matter-of-fact voice and meet more and more people who no longer exist.

More fields of flowers appear, followed by the evening's next program, also presenting photographs; but the people here are completely different. These are, for the most part, elderly men, sloppily dressed (with wrinkled collars and rumpled denim jackets), their desperate faces sunken and unshaven, some bearded. A big piece of cardboard with his name written on it hangs from the neck of each. When a particular face appears, one of the cardplayers exclaims, "Aha, so *that's* the one!" and everybody looks intently at the screen. The announcer is reading the personal data of each and the list of crimes that each committed. General Mohammed Zand gave the order to fire on an unarmed demonstration in Tabriz: hundreds were killed. Major Hossein Farzin tortured prisoners by burning their eyelids and pulling out their fingernails. A few hours ago, the announcer says, the firing squad of the Islamic Militia carried out the sentence of the tribunal against them.

The hall feels stuffy and oppressive during this parade of good then evil absent ones—all the more so because the wheel of death that's been turning for so long keeps spinning and throwing off hundreds of new people (faded photographs and ones just taken, graduation pictures, prison mug shots). This procession of still, silent faces flowing past in fits and starts becomes depressing but at the same time so absorbing that I expect suddenly to see my cardplayers' faces on the screen, then my own, and hear the announcer reading our names.

I walk back upstairs, through the empty corridor, and lock myself in my cluttered room. As usual at this hour I can hear gunfire from the depths of an invisible city. The shooting starts regularly at nine as if custom or tradition had fixed the hour. Then the city falls silent. Then there are more shots and muffled explosions. No one's upset, no one pays attention or feels directly threatened (no one except those who are shot). Since the middle of

February, when the uprising broke out in the city and the crowds seized the army munitions depots, Teheran has been armed, intensely charged, while in streets and houses, under cover of darkness, the drama of assassination is enacted. The underground keeps a low profile during the day, but at night it sends masked combat squads into the city.

These uneasy nights force people to lock themselves in their own homes. There is no curfew, but getting anywhere between midnight and dawn is difficult and risky. The Islamic Militia or the independent combat squads rule the looming, motionless city between those hours. Both are groups of well-armed boys who point their guns at people, cross-examine them, confer among themselves, and occasionally, just to be on the safe side, take those they've stopped to jail—from which it is difficult to get out. What's more, you are never sure who has locked you up, since no identifying marks differentiate the various representatives of violence whom you encounter, no uniforms or caps, no armbands or badges—these are simply armed civilians whose authority must be accepted unquestioningly if you care about your life. After a few days, though, we grow used to them and learn to tell them apart. This distinguished-looking man, in his well-made white shirt and carefully matched tie, walking down the street shouldering a rifle is certainly a militiaman in one of the ministries or central offices. On the other hand, this masked boy (a woolen stocking pulled over his head and holes cut out at eyes and mouth) is a local fedayeen no one's supposed to know by sight or name. We can't be sure about these people dressed in green U.S. Army fatigue jackets, rushing by in cars, barrels of guns pointed out the windows. They might be from the militia, but then again they might belong to one of the opposition combat groups (religious fanatics, anarchists, last remnants of Savak) hurrying with suicidal determination to carry out an act of sabotage or revenge.

But finally it's no fun trying to predict just whose ambush is awaiting you, whose trap you'll fall into. People don't like surprises, so they barricade themselves in their homes at night. My hotel is also locked (at this hour the sound of gunfire mingles with the creaking of shutters rolling down and the slamming shut of gates and doors). No friends will drop by; nothing like that will happen. I have no one to talk to. I'm sitting alone looking through notes and pictures on the table, listening to taped conversations.

DAGUERREOTYPES

Photograph I

Here's the oldest picture I've managed to obtain. A soldier, holding a chain in his right hand, and a man, at the end of the chain. The two gaze intently into the lens. This is clearly an important moment in their lives. The soldier is an older man, on the short side, a simple, obedient peasant, wearing an oversized, clumsily stitched uniform, trousers rumpled like an accordion, a big cap tilted onto protruding ears—in sum, an amusing figure reminiscent of the good soldier Schweik. The man on the chain: thin, pale face, sunken eyes, bandaged head, obviously wounded. The photo's caption says the soldier is the grandfather of Shah Mohammed Reza Pahlavi (the last Shah of Iran) and the wounded man is the assassin of Shah Nasr-ed-Din. Accordingly, the photo must date from 1896, when Nasr-ed-Din, after reigning for forty-nine years, was killed. The grandfather and the murderer look tired, which is understandable, since they have been wandering for days from Qom to the place of public execution in Teheran. They have been trudging down the desert road in scorching heat and stifling air, the soldier at the rear and the gaunt killer before him on his chain, like a member of an old-time circus troupe and his trained bear working their way from village to village, earning food for themselves. At times the assassin complains about the pain in his injured head but for the most part they are silent, because finally they have nothing to talk about. The murderer has killed, and the grandfather is leading him to his execution. Persia is a country of extreme poverty; it has no railroads, only the aristocracy own horse-drawn conveyances, and thus these two men must walk to the distant goal established by sentence and order. From time to time they come across a few clay huts where haggard peasants surround the dusty travelers. "Who is that you're leading, sir?" they shyly ask the soldier. "Who?" the soldier repeats the question and holds his tongue for a moment to heighten the suspense. "This," he says finally, pointing to the prisoner, "is the Shah's murderer." The grandfather's voice betrays a note of unconcealed pride. The peasants gape at the assassin in horror and admiration. Because he's killed someone great, he also seems somehow great. His crime has elevated him to a higher realm of existence. The peasants cannot decide between glowering indignantly and falling to their knees. Meanwhile, the soldier ties the chain to a stake driven into the ground at the roadside, unslings his rifle (which is so long, it almost touches the ground when slung over his shoulder), and orders the peasants to bring water and food. They scratch their heads. There is almost nothing to eat in the village, because a famine is raging. We should add that the soldier himself is a peasant, just like them, and no more than they does he even have a surname of his own—he calls himself Savad-Kuhi, the name of his village—but he has a carbine and a uniform and has been singled out to lead the Shah's assassin to the place of execution, so he takes advantage of his high position and again commands the peasants to bring water and food, since he is excruciatingly hungry and, furthermore, cannot allow the man on the chain to perish of thirst or exhaustion. If that happened, the extraordinary spectacle of hanging the Shah's assassin in a crowded Teheran square would have to be canceled. Badgered ruthlessly by the soldier, the peasants end up bringing what they themselves would have eaten: withered rootlets dug from the ground and a canvas pouch full of dried locusts. The grandfather and the murderer sit down in the shade to eat, eagerly popping locusts into their mouths, spitting out the wings, and washing the remains down with water, while the peasants look on in silent envy. As evening draws near, the soldier chooses the best hut, throws out its owners, and turns it into a temporary jail. He winds the prisoner's chain around his own body, then, tired from countless hours of marching under the blazing sun, the two stretch out on the clay floor black with cockroaches and fall into deep sleep. In the morning they get up and continue on the road to the goal established by sentence and order, northward, to Teheran, across the same desert, in the same quivering heat, the murderer with his bandaged head, his long swinging tail of iron chain held up by the hand of the escorting soldier, in his clumsily sewn uniform, looking so comical with his large cap resting askew on his protruding ears that when I first saw him in this photo I thought it was Schweik himself.

Photograph 2

Here we see a young officer of the Persian Cossack Brigade standing next to a machine gun and explaining the principles of the deadly weapon to his colleagues. This particular weapon is the updated 1910 model of the

Maxim gun, so the photograph must be from about that year. The young officer, named Reza Khan and born in 1878, is the son of the soldier-escort we met leading the Shah's murderer across the desert less than two decades earlier. If we compare the two pictures, we immediately notice that Reza Khan, unlike his father, is a physical giant. He is taller than his colleagues by at least a head, has a bulging chest, and looks like the sort of muscleman who could break a horseshoe with ease. He has a military mien, a cold, piercing look, a wide, massive jaw, and clenched lips on which even the faintest smile would be out of the question. On his head sits a broad cap of black caracul, for he is, as I have mentioned, an officer of the Persian Cossack Brigade (the only army that the Shah of those days had) commanded by Vsevolod Lyakhov, a Tsarist colonel from St. Petersburg. Reza Khan is the protégé of Colonel Lyakhov, who has a fondness for born soldiers, and our young officer is the model of the born soldier. He joined the Brigade as an illiterate boy of fourteen (he will never learn to read and write well) and climbed gradually through the echelons of professional soldiery thanks to his obedience, discipline, decisiveness, innate intelligence, and what the military likes to call leadership quality. Great promotions come his way only after 1917, however, when the Shah, (quite mistakenly) suspecting Lyakhov of Bolshevik sympathies, sends him back to Russia. Now Reza Khan becomes a colonel and the commander of the Cossack Brigade, which soon falls under British protection. At a reception the British general Sir Edmund Ironside stands on tiptoe to reach Reza Khan's ear and whispers, "Colonel, you are a man of great possibilities." They walk out into the garden where the general, in the course of their stroll, suggests a *coup d'état* and conveys London's blessings. In February, 1921, Reza Khan enters Teheran at the head of his brigade, arrests the capital's politicians (it is winter, snow is falling; the politicians will later complain about their cold damp cells), and forms a new government, in which he serves first as Minister of War and then as Prime Minister. In December, 1925, the obedient Constitutional Assembly (which fears the colonel and the Englishmen standing behind him) proclaims the cossack commander Shah of Persia. From now on our young officer—in the photograph explaining the principles of the updated 1910-model Maxim machine gun to his colleagues (all wearing belted Russian peasant shirts and quilted jackets)—will be known as Shah Reza the Great, King of Kings, Shadow of the Almighty, God's Vicar and the Center of the Universe, and also as founder of the Pahlavi dynasty, which begins with him and, destiny decrees, ends with his son, who, on a winter morning as chilly as the day his father seized power and throne, fifty-eight years later, will depart the palace and Teheran, by jet, to an ambiguous fate.

Photograph 3

Whoever scrutinizes this photo of father and son, taken in 1926, will understand a lot. The father is forty-eight and the son seven. The contrast between them is striking in every respect: The huge, powerful Shah-father stands sulkily, peremptorily, hands on his hips, and beside him the small pale boy, frail, nervous, obediently standing at attention, barely reaches his father's waist. They are wearing the same uniforms and caps, the same shoes and belts, and the same number of buttons: fourteen. The father, who wants his son—so essentially unlike him—to resemble him in as many details as possible, thought up this identity of apparel. The son senses this intention, and, though he is by nature weak and hesitant, he will try at all costs to resemble his despotic, ruthless father. From that moment two natures begin to develop and coexist in the boy: the inborn one and the parental one that, because of his ambitions, he starts to acquire. Finally he falls so totally under his father's domination that when he becomes Shah many years later, he automatically (but also, often, consciously) repeats Daddy's behavior and even, toward the end of his reign, invokes his father's authority. But at this moment the father is assuming power with all his inborn energy and drive. He has an acute sense of mission and knows what he is after—in his own brutal words, he wants to put the ignorant mob to work and build a strong modern state before which all will beshit themselves in fear. His are the Prussian's iron hand, the slavedriver's simple methods. Ancient, slumbering, loafing Iran (on the Shah's orders, Persia will hereafter be called Iran) trembles to its foundations. He begins by creating an imposing army. A hundred and fifty thousand men get uniforms and guns. The army is the apple of the Shah's eye, his great passion. The army must always have money. It must have everything. The army will make the nation modern, disciplined, obedient. Everyone: *Attention!* The Shah issues an order forbidding Iranian dress. Everyone, wear European suits! Everyone, don European hats! The Shah bans chadors. In the streets, police tear them off terrified women. The faithful protest in the mosques of Meshed. He sends in the artillery to level the mosques and massacre the rebels. He or-

22

ders that the nomadic tribes be settled permanently. The nomads protest. He orders their wells poisoned, threatening them with death by thirst and starvation. The nomads keep protesting, so he sends out punitive expeditions that turn vast regions into uninhabited land. A lot of blood flows. He forbids the photographing of that symbolically backward beast, the camel. In Qom a mullah preaches a critical sermon, so, armed with a cane, the Shah enters the mosque and pummels the critic. He imprisons the great Ayatollah Madresi, who had raised his voice in complaint, in a dungeon for years. The liberals protest timorously in the newspapers, so the Shah closes down the newspapers and imprisons the liberals. He orders several of them walled up in a tower. Those he considers malcontents must report daily to the police. Aristocratic ladies faint in terror at receptions when this gruff unapproachable giant turns his harsh gaze on them. Until the end Reza Khan preserves many of the habits of his village childhood and his barracks youth. He lives in a palace but still sleeps on the floor; he always goes around in uniform; he eats with his soldiers from the same pot. One of the boys! At the same time, he covets land and money. Taking advantage of his power, he accumulates incredible wealth. He becomes the biggest landowner, proprietor of nearly three thousand villages and the two hundred and fifty thousand peasants living in them; he owns stock in factories and banks, receives tribute, counts, totes, adds, calculates—if a splendid forest, green valley, or fertile plantation so much as catches his eye, it must be his—indefatigably, insatiably he increases his estates, multiplying his enormous fortune. No one may even approach the borders of the Shah's lands. One day there is a public execution: On the Shah's orders a firing squad kills a donkey that, ignoring all warning signs, entered a meadow belonging to Reza Khan. Peasants from neighboring villages are herded to the place of execution to learn respect for the master's property. But apart from his cruelty, greed, and outlandishness, the old Shah deserves credit for saving Iran from the dissolution that threatened after the First World War. In his efforts to modernize the country he built roads and railways, schools and offices, airports and new residential quarters in the cities. The nation remained poor and apathetic, however, and when Reza Khan departed, an exultant people celebrated the event for a long time.

Photograph 4

Here's a picture that circulated around the world in its time: Stalin, Roosevelt, and Churchill sitting in armchairs on a spacious veranda. Stalin and Churchill are wearing uniforms, Roosevelt a dark suit. Teheran, a sunny December morning, 1943. Everybody in this picture is putting on a serene face meant to cheer us; after all, we know that the worst war in history is underway and the expression on these faces is crucial: It has to encourage us. The photographers finish, and the three great ones move into the hall for a moment of private conversation. Roosevelt asks Churchill what has become of the ruler of this country, Shah Reza (if, Roosevelt adds, I'm pronouncing it correctly). Churchill shrugs his shoulders and speaks reluctantly. The Shah admired Hitler and surrounded himself with Hitler's people. There were Germans all over Iran, in the palace, the ministries, the army. The Abwehr became a force to reckon with in Teheran, and the Shah looked on approvingly—Hitler was at war with England and Russia, and our monarch could not tolerate England and Russia; he rubbed his hands gleefully as the Führer's armies advanced. London was worried about Iranian oil, which fueled the British fleet, and Moscow was afraid the Germans would land in Iran and attack in the region of the Caspian Sea. But the major concern remained the trans-Iranian railroad, which the Americans and the British needed to transport food and weapons to Stalin. Then, at a moment of crisis, as German divisions were advancing farther and farther eastward, the Shah suddenly refused the Allies use of the railroad. They moved decisively: Units of the British and Red armies entered Iran in August, 1941. The Shah received with disbelief, as a personal humiliation and defeat, news that fifteen Iranian divisions had surrendered without much resistance. Some of his troops dispersed and went home, while others were locked up in their barracks by the Allies. Deprived of his soldiers the Shah no longer mattered, no longer existed. The British, who respect even those monarchs who betray them, left Reza Khan an honorable way out: Would His Highness kindly abdicate in favor of his son, the heir to the throne? We have a high opinion of him and will ensure his position. But His Highness should not think there is any other solution. The Shah agreed and in September of that year, 1941, his twenty-two-year-old son Mohammed Reza Pahlavi ascended the throne. The old autocrat was a private person now, and for the first time in his adult life he put on civilian clothes. The British sent him to Africa, to Johannesburg (where he died after three years of a dull, comfortable life about which there is not much to say). Empire giveth; empire taketh away.

From the Notes 1

I see I'm missing or have misplaced a few pictures. I don't have the shots of the last Shah in his early youth. I don't have the one from 1939 when he was attending officers' school in Teheran: On his twentieth birthday his father promoted him to general. I don't have a picture of his first wife, Fawzia, bathing in milk. Yes, Fawzia, King Farouk's sister and a girl of striking beauty, bathed in milk—but Princess Ashraf, the young Shah's twin sister and, as some say, his evil genius, his black conscience, poured caustic detergent into the bathtub: yet another palace scandal. But I do have a picture of the last Shah on September 16, 1941, when he succeeded his father and was crowned Shah Mohammed Reza Pahlavi. Slender, in a dress uniform, a sword at his side, he is standing in the chambers of parliament and reading the text of the oath from a sheet of paper. This picture was repeated in all the published commemorative albums devoted to the Shah, of which there were scores, if not hundreds. He loved reading books about himself and looking through albums published in his honor. He loved unveiling his monuments and portraits. Catching a glimpse of the monarch's likeness was nearly unavoidable. To stand in any given place and open your eyes was enough: The Shah was everywhere. Since height was not his strong point, photographers always shot from angles that made him seem the tallest person in the picture. He furthered this illusion by wearing elevator shoes. His subjects kissed his shoes. I have just such a picture, where they are prostrating themselves and kissing his elevator shoes. On the other hand, I don't have a photo of a certain uniform of his, from 1949. That apparel, pocked with bullet holes and stained with blood, was displayed in a glass case at the officers' club in Teheran as relic and reminder. The Shah was wearing it when a young man pretending to be a photographer but with a gun built into his camera got off a series of shots that wounded the monarch gravely. There were five attempts on his life, in all. Thus around him grew an atmosphere of danger (finally real), and he had to be surrounded by policemen wherever he went. The Iranians resented the fact that, for security reasons, only foreigners were invited to certain celebrations in which the Shah took part. His compatriots also said bitingly that since he traveled almost exclusively by airplane and helicopter, he saw his country only from a lofty vantage point that obliterated all contrasts. I don't have any photographs of Khomeini in his early years. When he appears in my collection, he is already an old man, and so it is as if he had never been young or middle-aged. The local fanatics believe Khomeini is the Twelfth Imam, the Awaited One, who disappeared in the ninth century and has now returned, more than a thousand years later, to deliver them from misery and persecution. That Khomeini almost always appears in photographs only as an aged man could be taken as confirmation of this belief.

Photograph 5

This is undoubtedly the greatest day in the long life of Doctor Mossadegh. He is leaving parliament high on the shoulders of an elated crowd. He is smiling and holding up his right hand in greeting to the people. Three days earlier, on April 28, 1951, he became Prime Minister, and today parliament has passed his bill nationalizing the country's oil. Iran's greatest treasure has become the property of the nation. We have to enter into the spirit of that epoch, because the world has changed a great deal since. In those days, to dare the sort of act that Doctor Mossadegh just performed was tantamount to dropping a bomb suddenly and unexpectedly on Washington or London. The psychological effect was the same: shock, fear, anger, outrage. Somewhere in Iran, some old lawyer who must be a half-cocked demagogue has pillaged Anglo-Iranian—the pillar of the Empire! Unheard of, unforgiveable! In those years, colonial property was a sacred value, the ultimate taboo. But that day, whose exalted atmosphere the faces in the photograph reflect, the Iranians do not yet know they have committed a crime for which they will have to suffer bitter painful punishment. Right now, all Teheran is living joyous hours of its great day of liberation from a foreign and hated past. Oil is our blood! the crowds chant enthusiastically. Oil is our freedom! The palace shares the mood of the city, and the Shah signs the act of nationalization. It is a moment when all feel like brothers, a rare instant that quickly turns into a memory because accord in the national family is not going to last long. Mossadegh never had good relations with the Pahlavis, father and son. Mossadegh's ideas had been formed by French culture: A liberal and a democrat, he believed in institutions like parliament and a free press and lamented the state of dependence in which his homeland found itself. The fall of Reza Khan presented a great opportunity for him and those like him. The young monarch, meanwhile, takes more interest in good times and sports than in politics, so there is a chance for democracy in Iran, a chance for the country to win full independence. Mossadegh's power is so great and his slogans are so popular that the Shah ends up on the sidelines. He plays soccer, flies his private airplane, organizes masked balls, divorces and remarries, and goes skiing in Switzerland.

Photograph 6

Here are the Shah and his new wife Soraya Esfandiari in Rome. But this is no honeymoon, no fun-filled carefree adventure far from the worries and routines of everyday life; no, this is their exile. Even in this posed shot the thirty-four-year-old Shah (tanned, dressed in a light double-breasted suit) cannot hide his edginess—small wonder, since he doesn't know whether he is going to return to the throne he left so hurriedly, or lead the life of an emigré wandering the globe. Soraya, a woman of conspicuous but cold beauty, daughter of the tribal leader of the Bakhtiars and of a German woman who settled in Iran, looks more in control: Her face reveals little, especially with dark glasses hiding her eyes. Yesterday, August 17, 1953, they flew here from their homeland in their own airplane (with the Shah at the controls; flying always relaxed him) and checked into the swank Hotel Excelsior, to which dozens of paparazzi have flocked to immortalize each appearance by the imperial couple. Rome is full of tourists in this summer vacation season and the Italian beaches are packed (the bikini is just coming into fashion). Europe is resting, vacationing, sightseeing, dining well in good restaurants, hiking in the mountains, pitching tents, gathering strength for the chill autumn and snowy winter. Teheran, in the meantime, has neither calm moments nor relaxation because everyone can already smell the gunpowder and hear the knives being sharpened. Everyone is saying that something must happen, will happen (everyone senses the wearying pressure of ever thickening air portending explosion), but only a handful of conspirators knows who will begin it and how. Doctor Mossadegh's two years of rule are drawing to a close. Constantly threatened with coups (the democrats, the liberals, the Shah's people, and the Islamic fanatics all are plotting against him), the Doctor has transferred his bed, a briefcase full of pajamas (he is used to working in his pajamas), and a bag full of medicines to parliament, where he thinks he will be safe. He lives and works here, never venturing out, already so broken that those who visit him always tell of the tears in his eyes. All his hopes have vanished, all his calculations have proven wrong. He has eliminated the English from the oilfields, for each nation has the right to its own resources, but he forgot that might makes right. The West proclaims a blockade of Iran and a boycott of the country's oil, which becomes forbidden fruit on the world market. The Shah cannot decide: Should he obey those officers closest to the palace who are advising him to eliminate Mossadegh so as to save the monarchy and the army? For a long time he has been unable to take the final step that would burn once and for all his flimsy bridges to the Prime Minister (they are bound in a struggle that admits of no compromise because it is the conflict between two principles: the autocracy of the Shah and the democracy of Mossadegh), and perhaps the Shah is continuing to delay because he feels some sort of respect for the old Doctor, or perhaps simply because, unsure of himself, of his own will to uncompromising action, he lacks the courage to declare war on Mossadegh. The Shah would doubtless prefer that someone else carry out the whole painful, even brutal operation for him. Still undecided and continually anguished, he travels from Teheran to his summer residence in Ramsar on the Caspian Sea, where in the end he signs a sentence against the Prime Minister. But when it develops that the first attempt to finish off the Doctor has come to light and ended in a setback for the palace, the Shah does not wait for further (and, as it turns out, favorable) events but instead flees to Rome with his young bride. He returns to Teheran a few weeks later, only after the army has deposed Mossadegh and delivered all authority into the monarch's hands.

Cassette 1

Yes, of course—you can record. Today he is no longer a prohibited subject. Before, he was. Do you know that for twenty-five years it was forbidden to utter his name in public? That the name "Mossadegh" was purged from all books, all history texts? And just imagine: Today, young people, who, it was assumed, should know nothing about him, go to their deaths carrying his portrait. There you have the best proof of what such expunging and rewriting history leads to. But the Shah didn't understand that. He did not understand that even though you can destroy a man, destroying him does not make him cease to exist. On the contrary, if I can put it this way, he begins to exist all the more. These are paradoxes no tyrant can deal with. The scythe swings, and at once the grass starts to grow back. Cut again and the grass grows faster than ever. A very comforting law of nature. Mossadegh! The English nicknamed him "Old Mossy." He drove them crazy, and yet they respected him in a way. No Englishman ever took a shot at him. In the end it was necessary to summon our own uniformed goons. And it took them only a few days to establish their kind of order! Mossy went off to prison for three years. Five thousand people went up against the wall or died in the streets—the price of rescuing the throne. A sad, bloody, dirty re-entry. You ask if Mossy was fated to lose? He didn't lose. He won. Such a man can't be erased from people's memories; so he can be thrown out of office but never out of history. The memory is a private possession to which no authority has access. Mossy said the land we walk on belongs to us and everything we find in that land is ours. Nobody in this country had ever put it that way. He also said, Let everybody speak out—I want to hear their ideas. Do you understand this? After two and a half millennia of tyrannical degradation he pointed out to the Iranian that he is a thinking being. No ruler had ever done that! People remembered what Mossy said. It stayed in their minds and remains alive to this day. Words that open our eyes to the world are always the easiest to remember. And so it was with those words. Could anyone say that Mossy was wrong in what he did and said? Today everyone says that he was right, but that the problem is he was right too early. You can't be right too early, because then you risk your own career and at times your own life. It takes a long time for a truth to mature, and in the meantime people suffer or blunder around in ignorance. But suddenly along comes a man who speaks that truth too soon, before it has become universal, and then the ruling powers strike out at the heretic and burn him at the stake or lock him up or hang him because he threatens their interests or disturbs their peace. Mossy came out against the monarchical dictatorship and against the country's subjugation. Today monarchies are falling one after the other and subjugation has to be masked with a thousand disguises because it arouses such opposition. But he came out against it thirty years ago, when nobody here dared say these obvious things. I saw him two weeks before his death. When was that?

It must have been in February, '67. He had spent the last ten years of his life under house arrest on a little farm outside Teheran. Visiting him was forbidden, of course, and the police watched the whole area. But you can arrange anything in this country if you know the right people and have the money. Money changes all the iron rules into rubber bands. Mossy must have been close to ninety then. I think he lasted so long because he wanted to see the time when life would admit he had been right. He was a hard man, hard on others because he never wanted to back down. But such a man couldn't back down even if he wished to. Until the end he thought clearly and knew exactly what was going on. Yet he could get around only with difficulty, leaning on a cane. He would stop and lie down on the ground to rest. The police who watched him said later that he was out walking like that one morning and lay down on the ground to rest, but he stayed there for a long time and when they went up to him they could see he was dead.

From the Notes 2

Oil kindles extraordinary emotions and hopes, since oil is above all a great temptation. It is the temptation of ease, wealth, strength, fortune, power. It is a filthy, foul-smelling liquid that squirts obligingly up into the air and falls back to earth as a rustling shower of money. To discover and possess the source of oil is to feel as if, after wandering long underground, you have suddenly stumbled upon royal treasure. Not only do you become rich, but you are also visited by the mystical conviction that some higher power has looked upon you with the eye of grace and magnanimously elevated you above others, electing you its favorite. Many photographs preserve the moment when the first oil spurts from the well: people jumping for joy, falling into each other's arms, weeping. Oil creates the illusion of a completely changed life, life without work, life for free. Oil is a resource that anesthetizes thought, blurs vision, corrupts. People from poor countries go around thinking: God, if only we had oil! The concept of oil expresses perfectly the eternal human dream of wealth achieved through lucky accident, through a kiss of fortune and not by sweat, anguish, hard work. In this sense oil is a fairy tale and, like every fairy tale, a bit of a lie. Oil fills us with such arrogance that we begin believing we can easily overcome such unyielding obstacles as time. With oil, the last Shah used to say, I will create a second America in a generation! He never created it. Oil, though powerful, has its defects. It does not replace thinking or wisdom. For rulers, one of its most alluring qualities is that it strengthens authority. Oil produces great profits without putting a lot of people to work. Oil causes few social problems because it creates neither a numerous proletariat nor a sizable bourgeoisie. Thus the government, freed from the need of splitting the profits with anyone, can dispose of them according to its own ideas and desires. Look at the ministers from oil countries, how high they hold their heads, what a sense of power they have, they, the lords of energy, who decide whether we will be driving cars tomorrow or walking. And oil's relation to the mosque? What vigor, glory, and significance this new wealth has given to its religion, Islam, which is enjoying a period of accelerated expansion and attracting new crowds of the faithful.

From the Notes 3

He says that what later happened with the Shah was quintessentially Iranian. Since time immemorial the reigns of every monarch have ended in lamentable, shameful ways. They died beheaded or with knives in their backs or—if they were luckier—had to flee the country, to die, exiled, abandoned, forgotten. He does not remember, although there may have been such exceptions, a Shah ending his days on the throne surrounded by respect and love, dying a natural death. He cannot remember the nation weeping for one of its rulers and bearing him to the grave with tearful eyes. In the last century all the Shahs, and there were quite a few of them, lost their crowns and their lives in unpleasant circumstances. The people regarded them as monsters, denounced their vilenesses, accompanied their departures with the curses and abuse of the crowd, and made news of their deaths the occasion for joyful holidays.

Of course, he says, we have had excellent Shahs like Cyrus and Abbas, but that was long ago. The last two dynasties spilled a great deal of innocent blood in order to win or keep the throne. Imagine the monarch Agha Mohammed Khan, who orders the entire population of the city of Kerman murdered or blinded—no exceptions. His praetorians set energetically to work. They line up the inhabitants, slice off the heads of the adults, gouge out the eyes of the children. In the end, despite taking regular breaks, the praetorians grow too exhausted to lift their swords or knives anymore. Only thanks to this fatigue do a remnant of the people preserve their lives and eyesight. Later, processions of blinded children leave the city. Some, wandering around the countryside, lose their way in the desert and die of thirst. Other groups reach inhabited settlements and, singing songs about the extermination of the citizens of Kerman, beg for food. News travels slowly in these days, so the people they meet are shocked to hear a chorus of barefoot, blinded children singing about whistling swords and tumbling heads. They ask what crime Kerman committed to earn such cruel punishment. At that question, the children break into a song about the offense, which was this: Because their fathers had sheltered the previous Shah, the new ruler could not forgive them. The spectacle of processions of blinded children arouses universal pity and the people do not refuse them sustenance, but the wanderers have to be fed discreetly and even secretly, since the little blinded ones, having been punished and stigmatized by the Shah, constitute a sort of peripatetic opposition and all support for the opposition is punishable to the highest degree. Gradually, sighted urchins attach themselves to these processions as guides for the blind children. Then they wander together, seeking food and protection from the cold and carrying the tale of the destruction of Kerman to the farthest villages.

These, he says, are the grim and brutal histories we hoard in our national memory. Tyrants won the throne by force, climbing toward it over corpses, amid maternal lamentations and the moans of the mortally wounded. The issue of succession was often settled in distant capitals, and the new pretender to the crown would enter Teheran with the British and Russian envoys supporting his elbows on either side. People treated such Shahs as usurpers and occupiers, and when one knows about that tradition one can understand how the mullahs managed to spark off so many uprisings against them. The mullahs would say: He, the one sitting in the palace, is a foreigner taking his orders from foreign powers. He is causing all your miseries; he's making a fortune at your expense and selling out the country. The people paid attention to this because the words of the mullahs struck them as the most obvious truths. I don't mean that the mullahs were saints. Far from it! Many dark forces lurk in the shadows of the mosque. But the abuses of power and the lawlessness of the palace made the mullahs into advocates of the national interest.

He returns to the fate of the last Shah. Back then, in Rome during his exile of a few days, Mohammed Reza has to face the fact that he could lose the throne forever and swell the exotic regiment of dispossessed royalty. That thought sobers him up. He wants to cast off the life that he has been squandering amid pleasures and distractions. (Later, he writes in his book that in Rome the sainted Ali appeared to him in a dream and said: Return to your homeland so that you can save the nation.) Now a great ambition is born in him, a yearning to demonstrate his strength and superiority. This trait, too, my interlocutor says, is most Iranian. One Iranian will never yield to another. Each believes in his own superiority, wants to be first and foremost, wants to impose his own exclusive *I. I! I! I* know better, *I* have more, *I* can do everything. The world begins with me, *I* am the whole world in myself. *I! I!* (To demonstrate, he stands up, rears his head high, peering down at me with exaggerated, haughty, oriental pride in his eyes.) Any group of Iranians immediately organizes itself according to hierarchical principles. I'm first, you're second, you're third. The second and third ones don't go for that, but immediately start trying to nose ahead, intriguing and maneuvering to unseat number one. Number one has to dig in to keep on top.

Dig in and get out the automatic rifles!

Similar rules apply elsewhere—for example, in the family. Because the man has to be superior, the woman must be inferior. Outside the home I might be a nonentity, but under my own roof I make up for it—here I am everything. Here my power admits of no division, and the more numerous the family, the wider and mightier my authority. The more children, the better: They give a man more to rule over. He becomes the monarch of a domestic state, commanding respect and admiration, deciding the fate of his subjects, settling disputes, imposing his will, ruling. (He stops to see what sort of an impression he is making on me. I protest energetically: I oppose such stereotypes. I know many of his fellow countrymen who are modest and polite, who have never made me feel inferior.) Quite true, he agrees, but only because you don't threaten us. You're not playing our game of seeing whose *I* is superior. This game made it impossible to create any solid parties because quarrels about leadership always broke out immediately and everyone would want to set up his own party. But now, upon his return from Rome, the Shah too throws himself body and soul into the game of trying to be the supreme *I*.

Since losing face is a great humiliation, he tells me,

the Shah first of all tries to recoup his lost face. Imagine, under our system of values, a monarch—the father of his country—who flees at the most critical moment, and is shown buying jewelry with his wife! No, he has to erase that impression somehow. So when Zahedi, whose army has overthrown the Mossadegh government, sends the Shah a telegram saying that the tanks have done their job and it is safe for the monarch to return, the Shah first heads for Iraq to have himself photographed leaning on the tomb of Ali, patron saint of the Shiites.

A religious gesture—that's how to get back in our nation's good graces.

So the Shah returns, but Iran is still far from calm—students on strike, streets full of demonstrations, gun battles, funerals. In the army itself, conflicts, plots, contention. The monarch thinks it safer to stay in the palace; too many people want his head. He surrounds himself with his family, courtiers, and generals. Now, with Mossadegh out of the way, Washington starts sending big bucks and the Shah sets aside half of the take for the military.

So the soldiers get meat and bread. You have to remember how miserably our people live and what it means for a soldier to have meat and bread, how that raises him above others.

In those days there were children everywhere with big swollen bellies; they'd been eating only grass.

I remember a man who burned his child's eyelid with a cigarette. The eye puffed up with pus, and the face looked terrible. This man smeared his own arm with axle grease, so the arm swelled up and turned black. He only wanted people to feel sorry for him and his child, so that somebody would feed them.

The only toys of my childhood were stones. I pulled a stone with a string—I was the horse, and the stone was the Gilded Chariot of the Shah.

From the Notes 4

Every pretext, he says, was good for rising up against the Shah. The people wanted to get rid of the dictator, and they flexed their muscles whenever they had the chance.

Everybody looked toward Qom. That's the way it had always been in our history: Whenever there was unhappiness and a crisis, people always started listening for the first signals from Qom.

And Qom was rumbling.

This was when the Shah extended diplomatic immunity to all U.S. military personnel and their families. Our army was already full of American experts. And the mullahs came right out and said that the Shah's move offended the principle of sovereignty. Now, for the first time, Iran would hear Ayatollah Khomeini. Before that, no one knew of him—nobody but the people of Qom, that is. He was already over sixty, old enough to be the Shah's father. Later he would often call the ruler "son," but of course in an ironic and wrathful tone. Khomeini attacked him ruthlessly. My people, he would cry, don't trust him. He's not your man! He's not thinking of you—he's only thinking of himself and of the ones who give him orders. He's selling out our country, selling us all out! *The Shah must go!*

The police arrest Khomeini. Demonstrations begin in Qom. People call for his freedom. Next, other cities take to the streets—Teheran, Tabriz, Meshed, Isfahan. Then the Shah sends the army into the streets and the slaughter begins. (He stands up, stretches out his arms, and curls his hands as though gripping the stock of a machine gun. He squints his right eye and makes a machine-gun rattattat.) That, he says, was June, 1963. The uprising went on for five months. Democrats from Mossadegh's party and the clerics led it. More than ten thousand people were killed or wounded. Then came a few years of funereal but never total quiet since some sort of rebellion and fighting was already breaking out. Khomeini was thrown out of the country and went to live in Iraq, in An Najaf, in the greatest Shiite city, site of Caliph Ali's tomb.

Now I wonder just what conditions created Khomeini. In those days, after all, there were plenty of more important, better-known ayatollahs as well as prominent political opponents of the Shah. We were all writing protests, manifestos, letters, statements. Only a small group of intellectuals read them because such materials could not be printed legally and, besides, most people didn't know how to read. We were criticizing the monarch, saying things were bad, demanding changes, reform, democratization, and justice. It never entered anyone's head to come out the way Khomeini did—to reject all that scribbling, all those petitions, resolutions, proposals. To stand before the people, and cry, *The Shah must go!*

That was the gist of what Khomeini said then, and he kept on saying it for fifteen years. It was the simplest thing, and everyone could remember it—but it took them fifteen years to understand what it really meant. After all, people took the institution of the monarchy as much

42

for granted as the air. No one could imagine life without it.

The Shah must go!

Don't debate it, don't gab, don't reform or forgive. There's no sense in it, it won't change anything, it's a vain effort, it's a delusion. We can go forward only over the ruins of the monarchy. There's no other way.

The Shah must go!

Don't wait, don't stall, don't sleep.

The Shah must go!

The first time he said it, it sounded like a maniac's entreaties, like the keening of a madman. The monarchy had not yet exhausted the possibilities of endurance.

Photograph 7

Here we see a group of people standing at a bus stop on a Teheran street. People waiting for a bus look the same all over the world, which is to say that they have the same tired, apathetic expression on their faces, the same posture of sluggishness and defeat, the same dullness and antipathy in their eyes. The man who gave me the photograph, whenever that was, asked me if I noticed anything strange in it. I thought it over and said, no, I couldn't spot anything. He replied that the picture had been taken under cover, from a window across the street. I was to note, he said as he showed it to me, the guy (with the anonymous face of a lower-level bureaucrat) standing near, inclining his ear toward three other men talking. That guy was from Savak and he was always on duty at the bus stop, eavesdropping as people waited for the bus and absent-mindedly bantered about this and that. People could discuss only innocuous matters, but even then it was necessary to stay away from subjects in which the police could pick out significant allusions. Savak had a good ear for all allusions. One scorching afternoon an old man with a bad heart turned up at the bus stop and gasped, "It's so oppressive you can't catch your breath." "So it is," the Savak agent replied immediately, edging closer to the winded stranger; "it's getting more and more oppressive and people are fighting for air." "Too true," replied the naive old man, clapping his hand over his heart, "such heavy air, so oppressive." Immediately, the Savak agent barked, "Now you'll have a chance to regain your strength," and marched him off. The other people at the bus stop had been listening in dread, for they had sensed from the beginning that the feeble elderly man was committing an unpardonable error by saying "oppressive" to a stranger. Experience had taught them to avoid uttering such terms as *oppressiveness, darkness, burden, abyss, collapse, quagmire, putrefaction, cage, bars, chain, gag, truncheon, boot, claptrap, screw, pocket, paw, madness,* and expressions like *lie down, lie flat, spreadeagle, fall on your face, wither away, gotten flabby, go blind, go deaf, wallow in it, something's out of kilter, something's wrong, all screwed up, something's got to give*—because all of them, these nouns, verbs, adjectives, and pronouns, could hide allusions to the Shah's regime, and thus formed a connotative minefield where you could get blown to bits with one slip of the tongue. For a moment, for just an instant, a new doubt flashed through the heads of the people standing at the bus stop: What if the sick old man was a Savak agent too? Because he had criticized the regime (by using "oppressive" in conversation), he must have been free to criticize. If he hadn't been, wouldn't he have kept his mouth shut or spoken about such agreeable topics as the fact that the sun was shining and the bus was sure to come along any minute? And who had the right to criticize? Only Savak agents, whose job it was to provoke reckless babblers, then cart them off to jail. The ubiquitous terror drove people crazy, made them so paranoid they couldn't credit anyone with being honest, pure, or courageous. After all, they considered themselves honest and yet they couldn't bring themselves to express an opinion or a judgment, to make any sort of accusation, because they knew punishment lay ruthlessly in wait for them. Thus, if someone verbally attacked and condemned the monarch, everybody thought he was an agent provocateur, acting maliciously to uncover those who agreed with him, to destroy them. The more incisively and lucidly he spoke the views that they kept hidden inside themselves, the more suspect he seemed and the more violently they backed away from him, warning their friends: Watch out, something fishy about this guy, he's acting too brave. In this way terror carried off its quarry—it condemned to mistrust and isolation anyone who, from the highest motives, opposed coercion. Fear so debased people's thinking, they saw deceit in bravery, collaboration in courage. This time, however, seeing how roughly the Savak agent led his victim away, the people at the bus stop had to admit that the ailing old man could not have been connected with the police. In any case, the captor and his prey were soon out of sight, and the sole remaining question was, Where did they go? Nobody actually knew where Savak was located. The organization had no headquarters. Dispersed all over the city (and all over the country), it was everywhere and nowhere. It occupied houses, villas, and apartments no one ever paid any attention to. Its doors stood blank or bore the names of nonexistent firms and institutions. Only those who were in on the secret knew its telephone numbers. Savak might rent quarters in an ordinary apartment house, or you might enter its interrogation rooms through a store, a laundry, a nightclub. In such a situation, all walls can have ears and every door or gate can lead to the secret police. Whoever fell into the grip of that organization disappeared without a trace, sometimes forever. People would vanish suddenly and nobody would know what had happened to them, where to go, whom to ask, whom to appeal to. They might be locked up in a prison, but which one? There were six thousand. An invisible, adamant wall would rise up, before which you stood helpless, unable to take a step forward. Iran belonged to Savak, but within the country the police acted like an underground organization that appeared then disappeared, hiding its tracks, leaving no forwarding address. Yet, at the same time, some of its sections existed officially. Savak censored the press, books, and films (it was Savak that banned the plays of Shakespeare and Molière because they criticized monarchical and aristocratic vices). Savak ruled in the universities, offices, and factories. A monstrously overgrown cephalopod, it entangled everything, crept into every crack and corner, glued its suckers everywhere, ferreted and sniffed in all directions, scratched and bored through every level of existence. Savak numbered sixty thousand agents. It also controlled, someone calculated, three million informants, who denounced other people from such varied motives as money, self-preservation, or the desire for a job or promotion. Savak bought people or condemned them to torture, appointed them to positions or clapped them into the dungeons. It defined the enemy and thus decided who should be destroyed. Of such a sentence there could be no review, no appeal. Only the Shah could save the condemned. Savak answered to the Shah alone, and those upon whom the monarchy rested quailed helplessly before the police. The people waiting at the bus stop knew all this and therefore remained silent once the Savak agent and the old man had gone. They watched each other out of the corners of their eyes, for all they knew the one standing next to them might have to inform. He might have just returned from an interview in which Savak told him that if by chance he noticed or heard something and reported it, his son would gain admission to the university. Or that if he noticed or heard something, the entry about his belonging to the opposition would be erased from the records. "For God's sake, I'm not in the opposition," he says in self-defense. "Yes you are; it's written down right here that you are." Without wanting to (even though some of them try to hide it so as not to provoke any aggressive outbursts), the people at the bus stop look at each other with loathing. They are inclined to neurotic, disproportionate reactions. Something gets on their nerves, something smells bad, and they move away from each other, waiting to see who goes after whom, who attacks someone first. This reciprocal distrust is the work of Savak, which has been whispering into all ears that everyone belongs to Savak. This one, this one, and that one. That one too? Sure, of course. Everybody. But on the other hand these people waiting for the bus might be decent folk, and their inward agitation, which they mask with silence and stony expressions, might stem from the fact that a moment earlier they felt the quick surge of fear that a close brush with Savak causes. Had their instinct failed them only for a moment, and had they begun discussing some ambiguous subject like the way that fish spoils quickly in the heat and the amazing fact that a rotting fish's head begins to stink first and has to be cut off immediately if you want to save the rest—had they broached such a culinary theme they might have shared the hapless lot of the man who held his hand over his heart. But they are safe for the moment and they stand at the bus stop wiping their sweat away and fanning their wet shirts.

From the Notes 5

Whisky sipped in conspiratorial circumstances (and you really have to conspire now, with Khomeini's prohibition in effect) has, like all forbidden fruits, an additional, enticing tang. Yet the glass holds just a few drops of liquid—the host has drawn his last bottle from deep in hiding and knows he won't be able to buy a next one. Iran's remaining alcoholics are dying: Unable to purchase vodka, wine, or beer, they gulp one of a variety of chemical solvents, which finishes them off.

We are sitting on the ground floor of a small, comfortable, well-cared-for townhouse, looking through the open glass doors onto the garden and the wall separating the property from the street. Ten feet high, this wall multiplies the territory of intimacy and constitutes a sort of outer boundary of the house, within which the living space has been built. My host and hostess are both around forty; they studied in Teheran and work in one of the travel agencies (of which, due to their compatriots' wanderlust, there are hundreds).

"We've been married more than twelve years," says the man, whose hair is just beginning to gray, "but only now, for the first time, have my wife and I been discussing politics. We'd never before spoken to each other on the subject. It's the same with all the other couples we know."

No, he doesn't want to imply they lacked faith in each other. Nor had they ever made any sort of agreement about the matter. Yet they had an unspoken compact that they accepted mutually and almost unconsciously, which resulted from a certain sober reflection on human nature: namely, that you never know how someone is going to behave in an extreme predicament, what he can be forced into, what calumny, what betrayal.

"The worst of it," his wife suggests, "is that no one can predict how much torture he'll be able to stand. And Savak meant, above all, torture of the most horrible kind. They would kidnap a man as he walked along the street, blindfold him, and lead him straight into the torture chamber without asking a single question. There they would start in with the whole macabre routine—breaking bones, pulling out fingernails, forcing hands into hot ovens, drilling into the living skull, and scores of other brutalities—in the end, when the victim had gone mad with pain and become a smashed, bloody mass, they would proceed to establish his identity. Name? Address? What have you been saying against the Shah? Come on, what have you been saying? And you know, he might not have said anything, ever. He might have been completely innocent. But to Savak, that was nothing, being innocent. This way everyone will be afraid, innocent and guilty alike, everyone will feel the intimidation, no one will feel safe. The terror of Savak depended on this ability to strike at everyone, on everyone's being accused, since accusations had to do not with deeds but with the sort of intentions that Savak could ascribe to anyone. Were you against the Shah? No, I wasn't. But you wanted to be, you shit! That was all it took.

"Sometimes they would hold a trial. For political acts (but what is a political act? Here, everything is a political act), they used only military courts: closed sessions, no counsel, no witnesses, and an instantaneous sentence. The execution took place later. Has anyone added up the number of people that Savak shot? Hundreds, for sure. Our great poet Khosrow Golesorkhi was shot. Our great director Keramat Denachian was shot. Dozens of writers, professors, and artists were imprisoned. Dozens of others had to emigrate to save themselves. Unbelievably ignorant and barbarous scum made up Savak, and when they got their hands on someone in the habit of reading books they worked him over with particular malice.

"Savak avoided trials and tribunals. They preferred other methods and did most of their killing in secret. Nothing could be established afterward. Who did the killing? Nobody knew. Who was guilty? There were no guilty ones.

"People went after the army and the police with their bare hands because they reached a point at which they could no longer stand the terror. It might look like desperation to you, but to us it was all the same.

"Do you know that if anyone mentioned Savak, whoever was talking to that person would look at him hours afterward and start thinking, Perhaps he's an agent? The one I was talking to might have been my father, my husband, my best friend. I would tell myself, Keep cool, it's nonsense, but nothing helped and the thought kept returning. Everything was sick—the whole regime was sick, and I have to say, I don't know when we will recover our health, our equilibrium. Years of a dictatorship like that broke us, psychologically, and I think it'll take a long long time before we can begin living normally."

Photograph 8

This picture was hanging alongside slogans, proclamations, and a few other photographs on the bulletin board in front of a revolutionary committee building in Shiraz. I asked a student to translate the handwritten statement thumbtacked below the photo. "It's written here," he said, "that this little boy, three years old, Habib Fardust, was a prisoner of Savak." "What?" I asked. "Three years old and a prisoner?" He answered that sometimes Savak locked up a whole family, which is what happened in this case. He read the statement to the end and added that the boy's parents had died during torture. Now, a lot of books are being published about Savak's crimes, along with various police documents and personal accounts by people who survived torture. And, the most shocking thing for me, I saw color postcards being sold in front of the university showing the bodies of Savak victims. Six hundred years after Tamburlaine, the same pathological cruelty remains, unchanged except perhaps for the degree of mechanization. The most common instrument discovered in Savak quarters was an electrically heated metal table called "the frying pan," on which the victim was tied down by his hands and feet. Many died on these tables. Often, the accused was already raving by the time he entered the torture chamber—few people could bear the screams they heard while they waited, and the smell of burning flesh. But technological progress could not displace medieval methods in this nightmare world. In Isfahan, people were thrown into huge bags full of cats crazed with hunger, or among poisonous snakes. Accounts of such horrors, sometimes, of course, propagated by Savak itself, circulated among the populace for years. They were so threatening, and the definition of an enemy of the state was so loose and arbitrary, that everyone could imagine ending up in such a torture chamber.

Photograph 9

This was taken in Teheran on December 23, 1973: The Shah, surrounded by a bank of microphones, is giving a speech in a hall crowded with journalists. On this occasion Mohammed Reza, usually marked by a careful, studied reticence, cannot hide his emotion, his excitement, even—as the reporters note—his feverishness. In fact, the moment is important and fraught with consequences for the whole world: The Shah is announcing a new price for oil. The price has quadrupled in less than two months, and Iran, which used to earn five billion dollars a year from its petroleum exports, will now be bringing in twenty billion. What's more, control of this great pile of money will belong to the Shah alone. In his autocratic kingdom he can use it however he likes. He can throw it into the sea, spend it on ice cream, or lock it up in a golden safe. No wonder he looks so excited—how would any of us behave if we suddenly found twenty billion dollars in our pockets and knew, additionally, there would be twenty billion more each and every year, and eventually even greater sums? No wonder the Shah acted as he did, which was to lose his head. Instead of assembling his family, loyal generals, and trusted advisers to think over together the most reasonable way of using such a fortune, the ruler—who claims to have suddenly been blessed with a shining vision— announces to one and all that within a generation he will make Iran (which is a backward, disorganized, half-illiterate, barefoot country) into the fifth greatest power on earth. At the same time the monarch awakens high hopes among his people with the attractive slogan "Prosperity for All." Initially, with everyone aware that the Shah is in the really big money, these hopes do not seem completely vain.

A few days after the press conference shown in our photograph, the monarch grants an interview to *Der Spiegel* and says, "In ten years we will have the same living standard that you Germans, French, and English have now."

"Do you think, sir," the correspondent asks incredulously, "you will be really able to accomplish this within ten years?"

"Yes, of course."

But, says the astonished journalist, the West needed many generations to achieve its present standard of living. Will you be able to skip all that?

Of course.

I think of this interview now, when Mohammed Reza is no longer in the country and, surrounded by half-naked shivering children, I am wading through mud and dung among the squalid clay huts of a little village outside Shiraz. In front of one of the huts a woman is forming cow patties into circular cakes that, once dried, will serve (in this country of oil and gas!) as the only fuel for her home. Well, walking through this sad medieval village and remembering that interview of a few years back, the most banal of reflections comes into my head: Not even the greatest nonsense is beyond the reach of human invention.

For the time being, however, the autocrat locks himself in his palace and begins issuing the hundreds of decisions that convulse his homeland and lead to his overthrow five years later. He orders investment doubled, begins the great importing of technology, and creates the third-most-advanced army in the world. He commands that the most up-to-date equipment be ordered, installed, and put in use. Modern machines produce modern merchandise, and Iran is going to swamp the world with its superior output. He decides to build atomic power plants, electronics factories, steel mills, and great industrial complexes. Then, since there is a delicious winter in Europe, he leaves to ski in St. Moritz. But his charming, elegant residence in St. Moritz suddenly stops being a quiet hideaway and retreat, because word of the new Eldorado has spread around the world by this time and excited the power centers, where everyone immediately has begun calculating the amounts of money to be plucked in Iran. The premiers and ministers of otherwise respectable and affluent governments from serious, respected countries have begun to line up outside the Shah's Swiss domicile. The ruler sat in an armchair, warming his hands at the fireplace and listening to a deluge of propositions, offers, and declarations. Now the whole world was at his feet. Before him were bowed heads, inclined necks, and outstretched hands. "Now look," he'd tell the premiers and ministers, "you don't know how to govern and that's why you don't have any money." He lectured London and Rome, advised Paris, scolded Madrid. The world heard him out meekly and swallowed even the bitterest admonitions because it couldn't take its eyes off the gold pyramid piling up in the Iranian desert. Ambassadors in Teheran went crazy under the barrage of telegrams that their ministers turned on them, all dealing with money: How much can the Shah give us? When and on what conditions? You say he won't? Then insist, Your Excellency! We offer guaranteed service and will ensure favorable publicity! Instead of elegance and seriousness, pushing and shoving without end, feverish glances and sweaty hands filled the waiting rooms of even the most petty Iranian ministers. People crowding each other, pulling at each other's sleeves, shouting, Get in line, wait your turn! These are the presidents of multinational corporations, directors of great conglomerates, representatives of famous companies, and finally the delegates of more or less respectable governments. One after another they are proposing, offering, pushing this or that factory for airplanes, cars, televisions, watches. And besides these notable and—under normal circumstances—distinguished lords of world capital and industry, the country is being flooded with smaller fry, penny-ante speculators and crooks, specialists in gold, gems, discotheques, strip joints, opium, bars, razor cuts, and surfing. These operators are scrambling to get into Iran, and they are unimpressed when, in some European airport, hooded students try to hand them pamphlets saying that people are dying of torture in their homeland, that no one knows whether the victims carried off by the Savak are dead or alive. Who cares, when the pickings are good and when, furthermore, everything is happening under the Shah's exulted slogan about building a Great Civilization? In the meantime, Mohammed Reza has returned from his winter vacation, well rested and satisfied. Everyone is praising him at last; the whole world is writing about him as an exemplar, puffing up his splendid qualities, constantly pointing out that everywhere, wherever you turn, there are so many foulups and cheats, whereas, in his land—not a one.

Unfortunately, the monarch's satisfaction is not to last long. Development is a treacherous river, as everyone who plunges into its currents knows. On the surface the water flows smoothly and quickly, but if the captain makes one careless or thoughtless move he finds out how many whirlpools and wide shoals the river contains. As the ship comes upon more and more of these hazards the captain's brow gets more and more furrowed. He keeps singing and whistling to keep his spirits up. The ship looks as if it is still traveling forward, yet it is stuck in one place. The prow has settled on a sandbar. All this, however, happens later. In the meantime the Shah is making purchases costing billions, and ships full of merchandise are steaming toward Iran from all the continents. But when they reach the Gulf, it turns out that the small obsolete ports are unable to handle such a mass of cargo (the Shah hadn't realized this). Several hundred ships line up at sea and stay there for up to six months, for which delay Iran pays the shipping companies a billion dollars annually. Somehow the ships are gradually unloaded, but then it turns out that there are no warehouses (the Shah hadn't realized). In the open air, in the desert, in nightmarish tropical heat, lie millions of tons of all sorts of cargo. Half of it, consisting of perishable foodstuffs and chemicals, ends up being thrown away. The remaining cargo now has to be transported into the depths of the country, and at this moment it turns out that there is no transport (the Shah hadn't realized). Or rather, there are a few trucks and trailers, but only a crumb in comparison to the need. Two thousand tractor-trailers are thus ordered from Europe, but then it turns out there are no drivers (the Shah hadn't realized). After much consultation, an airliner flies off to bring South Korean truckers from Seoul. Now the tractor-trailers start rolling and begin to transport the cargo, but once the truckdrivers pick up a few words of Farsi, they discover they're making only half as much as native truckers. Outraged, they abandon their rigs and return to Korea. The trucks, unused to this day, still sit, covered with sand, along the Bander Abbas–Teheran highway. With time and the help of foreign freight companies, however, the factories and machines purchased abroad finally reach their appointed destinations. Then comes the time to assemble them. But it turns out that Iran has no engineers or technicians (the Shah hadn't realized). From a logical point of view, anyone who sets out to create a Great Civilization ought to begin with people, with training cadres of experts in order to form a native intelligentsia. But it was precisely that kind of thinking that was unacceptable. Open new universities and polytechnics, every one a hornets' nest, every student a rebel, a good-for-nothing, a freethinker? Is it any wonder the Shah didn't want to braid the whip that would flay his own skin? The monarch had a better way—he kept the majority of his students far from home. From this point of view the country was unique. More than a hundred thousand young Iranians were studying in Europe and America. This policy cost much more than it would have taken to create national universities. But it guaranteed the regime a degree of calm and security.

The majority of these young people never returned. To-day more Iranian doctors practice in San Francisco or Hamburg than in Tebriz or Meshed. They did not return even for the generous salaries the Shah offered. They feared Savak and didn't want to go back to kissing anyone's shoes. An Iranian at home could not read the books of the country's best writers (because they came out only abroad), could not see the films of its outstanding directors (because they were not allowed to be shown in Iran), could not listen to the voices of its intellectuals (because they were condemned to silence). The Shah left people a choice between Savak and the mullahs. And they chose the mullahs. When thinking about the fall of any dictatorship, one should have no illusions that the whole system comes to an end like a bad dream with that fall. The physical existence of the system does indeed cease. But its psychological and social results live on for years, and even survive in the form of subconsciously continued behavior. A dictatorship that destroys the intelligentsia and culture leaves behind itself an empty, sour field on which the tree of thought won't grow quickly. It is not always the best people who emerge from hiding, from the corners and cracks of that farmed-out field, but often those who have proven themselves strongest, not always those who will create new values but rather those whose thick skin and internal resilience have ensured their survival. In such circumstances history begins to turn in a tragic, vicious circle from which it can sometimes take a whole epoch to break free. But we should stop here or even go back a few years, because by jumping ahead of events we have already destroyed the Great Civilization, and first we have to build it. And yet how do we build it here, where there are no experts and the nation, even if it is eager to learn, has nowhere to study? In order to fulfill his vision, the Shah needed at least 700,000 specialists immediately. Somebody hit upon the safest and best way out—import them. The issue of security carried great weight here since foreigners, concerned about doing their jobs, making money, and getting home, would clearly not organize plots and rebellions or contest and rail against Savak. In general, revolutions would stop breaking out around the world if, for example, Ecuadorans built Paraguay and Indians built Saudi Arabia. Stir, mix together, relocate, disperse, and you will have peace. Tens of thousands of foreigners thus begin arriving. Airplane after airplane land at Teheran airport: domestic servants from the Philippines, hydraulic engineers from Greece, electricians from Norway, accountants from Pakistan, mechanics from Italy, military men from the United States. Let us look at the pictures of the Shah from this period: He's talking to an engineer from Munich, a foreman from Milan, a crane operator from Boston, a technician from Kuznetsk. And who are the only Iranians in these pictures? Ministers and Savak agents guarding the monarch. Their countrymen, absent from the pictures, observe it all with ever-widening eyes. This army of foreigners, by the very strength of its technical expertise, its knowing which buttons to press, which levers to pull, which cables to connect, even if it behaves in the humblest way, begins to dominate and starts crowding the Iranians into an inferiority complex. The foreigner knows how, and I don't. This is a proud people, extremely sensitive about its dignity. An Iranian will never admit he can't do something; to him, such an admission constitutes a great shame and a loss of face. He'll suffer, grow depressed, and finally begin to hate. He understood quickly the concept that was guiding his ruler: All of you just sit there in the shadow of the mosque and tend your sheep, because it will take a century for you to be of any use! I on the other hand have to build a global empire in ten years with the help of foreigners. This is why the Great Civilization struck Iranians as above all a great humiliation.

Photograph 10

This is not exactly a photograph but rather a reproduction of an oil painting in which a panegyrist-dauber portrays the Shah in a Napoleonic pose (as when the French emperor, mounted, was directing one of his victorious battles). The Iranian Ministry of Information distributed this picture, and the Shah, who gloried in such comparisons, must therefore have approved. With galloons in giddy profusion, a plenitude of medals, and an intricate arrangement of cords across the chest, the well-cut uniform accentuates the attractive, athletic silhouette of Mohammed Reza. The image depicts him in his favorite role: commander of the army. The Shah, of course, always concerned himself with the welfare of his subjects, occupied himself with accelerated development, and so on, but these were all burdensome obligations resulting from the fact that he was the father of his country, while his true hobby, his real passion, was the army. Nor was this an entirely disinterested fascination. The army had always constituted the main prop of the throne and, as the years passed, it became more and more the sole support. At the moment that the army scattered, the Shah ceased to exist. And yet I hesitate to use the term "army," which can lead to mistaken associations—this was nothing but an instrument of domestic terror, a kind of police that lived in barracks. For this reason the nation looked upon any further development of the army with fear and terror, realizing that the Shah was swinging an ever thicker and more painful whip that would fall sooner or later across the backs of the people. The division between army and police (of which there were eight varieties) was merely formal. Army generals, intimates of the dictator, commanded each type of police. No less than Savak, the army enjoyed all the privileges. ("After studying in France," one doctor recalled, "I returned to Iran. My wife and I went to a movie and we were waiting on line to buy tickets. A noncomissioned officer appeared and went past everyone, straight to the box office. I made a remark about this. He walked back to me and slapped my face. I had to stand there and take it, because my neighbors in the line were warning me that any protest would land me in prison.") And so the Shah felt best in uniform and devoted the better part of his time to the military. For years his favorite occupation had been reading the magazines that the West produces in such profusion, displaying the newest varieties of weapons as advertised by their merchandisers and manufacturers. Mohammed Reza subscribed to all these periodicals and read them from cover to cover. For many years, before he had the money to buy every deadly toy that caught his fancy, he could only daydream, while engrossed in his reading, that the Americans would give him this tank or that airplane. And to be sure the Americans gave him a lot, but some Senator would always stand up to criticize the Pentagon for sending the Shah too many arms. Then the shipments would stop for a while. But now that the monarch was getting all that oil money, his problems were over. He immersed himself even more deeply in reading his magazines and arms catalogues. A stream of the most fantastic orders flowed out from Teheran. How many tanks does Great Britain have? Fifteen hundred? Fine, said the Shah—I'm ordering two thousand. How many artillery pieces does the Bundeswehr have? A thousand? Good, put us down for fifteen hundred. And why always more than the British army and the Bundeswehr? Because we've got to have the third-best army in the world. It's a shame that we can't have the first or the second, but the third is within reach and we're going to have it. So once again the ships steamed, the airplanes flew, and the trucks rolled in the direction of Iran bearing the most modern weapons that man could devise and produce. The more trouble it is to build factories, the more attractive the supply of tanks looks. So Iran quickly transforms itself into a great showplace for all types of weapons and military equipment. "Showplace" is the right word, because the country lacks the warehouses, magazines, and hangars to protect and secure it all. The spectacle has no precedent. If you drive from Shiraz to Isfahan even today you'll see hundreds of helicopters parked off to the right of the highway. Sand is gradually covering the inert machines.

Photograph 11

A Lufthansa airliner at Mehrabad airport in Teheran. It looks like an ad, but in this case no advertising is needed because all the seats are sold. This plane flies out of Teheran every day and lands at Munich at noon.

Waiting limousines carry the passengers to elegant restaurants for lunch. After lunch they all fly back to Teheran in the same airplane and eat their suppers at home.
Hardly an expensive entertainment, the jaunt costs only
two thousand dollars a head. For people in the Shah's
favor, such a sum is nothing. In fact, it is the palace
plebeians who only go to Munich for lunch. Those in
somewhat higher positions don't always feel like endur-
ing the travails of such long journeys. For them an Air
France plane brings lunch, complete with cooks and
waiters, from Maxim's of Paris. Even such fancies have
nothing extraordinary about them. They cost hardly a
penny when compared to a fairy-tale fortune like the one
that Mohammed Reza and his people are amassing. In
the eyes of the average Iranian the Great Civilization,
the Shah's Revolution, was above all a Great Pillage at
which the elite busied itself. Everyone in authority stole.
Whoever held office and did not steal created a desert
around himself; he made everybody suspicious. Other
people regarded him as a spy sent to report on who was
stealing how much, because their enemies needed such
information. Whenever possible they got rid of someone
like that in short order—he spoiled the game. All values
thus came to have a reversed meaning. Whoever tried
to be honest looked like a paid stoolie. If someone had
clean hands, he had to keep them deeply hidden because there was something shameful and ambivalent
about purity. The higher up, the fuller the pockets.
Anyone who wanted to build a factory, open a business,
or grow cotton had to give a piece of the action as a present to the Shah's family or one of the dignitaries. And
they gave willingly, because you could get a business
going only with the backing of the court. With money
and influence you would overcome every obstacle. You

could buy influence and use it afterward to multiply your fortune further. It is hard to imagine the river of money that flowed into the till of the Shah, his family, and the whole court elite. Bribes to the Shah's family generally ran to a hundred million dollars and more. Prime ministers and generals took bribes of from thirty to fifty million dollars. Lower down, the bribe was smaller, but it was always there! As prices rose, the bribes got bigger and ordinary people complained that more and more of their earnings went to feed the moloch of corruption. In earlier times Iran had known a custom of auctioning off positions. The Shah would announce a floor price for the office of governor and whoever bid highest became governor. Later, in office, the governor would plunder his subjects to recover (with interest) the money that had gone to the monarch. Now this custom was revived in a new form: The ruler would buy people by sending them to negotiate contracts, usually military ones.

The Shah's big money enabled him to breathe life into a new class, previously unknown to historians and sociologists: the petro-bourgeoisie. An unusual social phenomenon, the petro-bourgeoisie produces nothing, and unbridled consumption makes up its whole occupation. Promotion to this class depends on neither social conflict (as in feudalism) nor on competition (as in industry and trade), but only on conflict and competition for the Shah's grace and favor. This promotion can occur in the course of a single day, or even in a few minutes: The Shah's word or signature suffices. Whoever most pleases the ruler, whoever can best and most ardently flatter him, whoever can convince him of his loyalty and submission, receives promotion to the petro-bourgeoisie. This class of freeloaders quickly makes a significant part of the oil revenues its own and becomes proprietor

of the country. At their elegant villas its members en-
tertain visitors to Iran and shape their guests' opinions
of the country (though the hosts themselves often have
scant familiarity with their own culture). They have international manners and speak European languages—
what better reasons for the Europeans to depend on
them? But how misleading these encounters can be, how
far these villas are from the local realities that will soon
find a voice to shock the world! This class we are speaking about, guided by the instinct of self-preservation, has
premonitions that its own career will be as short-lived
as it is glittering. Thus, it sits on its suitcases from the
start, exporting money and buying property in Europe
and America. But since it has such big money, it can
earmark a part of its fortunes for a comfortable life at
home. Superluxurious neighborhoods, with enough
conveniences and ostentation to stupefy any sightseer,
begin to spring up in Teheran. Many of the houses cost
more than a million dollars. These neighborhoods take
root only a few streets away from districts where whole
families huddle in narrow, crowded hovels without elec-
tricity or running water. This privileged consumption,
this great hogging, should go on quietly and discreetly—take it, hide it, and leave nothing showing. Have
a feast, but draw the curtains first. Build for yourself,
but deep in the forest so as not to provoke others. So it
should be—but not here. Here, custom ordains that you
dazzle, knock the wind out of people, put everything on
display, light all the lights, stun them, bring them to their
knees, devastate them, pulverize them! Why have it at
all, if it's to be on the sly, some alleged thing that somebody has seen or heard about? No! To have it like that
is not to have it at all! To really have it is to blow your
horn, shout it, let others come and gawk at it until their

eyes pop out. And so, in plain sight of a silent and increasingly hostile people, the new class mounts an exhibition of the Iranian *dolce vita,* knowing no measure in its dissoluteness, rapacity, and cynicism. This provokes a fire in which the class itself, along with its creator and protector, will perish.

Photograph 12

This is a reproduction of a caricature that some opposition artist drew during the revolution. It shows a Teheran street. Big American cars, gas-guzzling roadhogs, are slinking along the avenue. On the sidewalks stand people with disappointed faces. Each of them is holding a part of a car: a door handle, fanbelt, or gearshift. The caption under the cartoon reads: "A Peykan for Everyone" (the Peykan is an Iranian economy car). When the Shah got into the big money he claimed that every Iranian would be able to buy his own car. The caricature shows how this pledge was fulfilled. Above the street, an angry Shah is sitting on a cloud with this inscription running above his head: "Mohammed Reza is furious with a nation that will not admit it feels an improvement." This is an interesting drawing, which tells how the Iranians interpreted the Great Civilization—as a Great Injustice. It created even bigger gulfs in a society that had never known equality. The Shahs, of course, had always had more than others, but it was hard to think of them as magnates. They had to sell concessions to keep the court in respectable shape. Shah Nasred-Din ran up such debts in Paris brothels that, in order to bail himself out and get back home, he sold the French the rights to carry out archaeological expeditions and keep whatever artifacts they found. But that was in the past. Now, in the mid-seventies, Iran has become a behemoth of riches. And what does the Shah do? Half the money goes to the army, some to the elite, the rest for development. But what does that word mean? "Development" is no indifferent, abstract concept. It always applies to someone, in the name of something. Development can make a society richer and life better, freer, more just—but it can also do exactly the opposite. So it is in autocratic societies (where the elite identifies its interests with those of the state that guarantees its control); in such societies, development, aiming at strengthening the state and its apparatus of repression, reinforces dictatorship, subjugation, barrenness, vagueness, and the emptiness of existence. The development packaged and sold in Iran as the Great Civilization worked in just that way. Can anyone blame the Iranians for rising up at the cost of great sacrifices and destroying that model of development?

From the Notes 6

A Shiite is, first of all, a rabid oppositionist. At first the Shiites were a small group of the friends and backers of Ali, the son-in-law of Mohammed and husband of the Prophet's beloved daughter Fatima. When Mohammed died without a male heir and without clearly designating his successor, the Muslims began struggling over the Prophet's inheritance, over who would be caliph, or leader of the believers in Allah and thus the most important person in the Islamic world. Ali's party

(*Shi'a* means "party") supports its leader for this position, maintaining that Ali is the sole representative of the Prophet's family, the father of Mohammed's two grandsons Hassan and Hussein. The Sunni Muslim majority, however, ignores the voices of the Shiites for twenty-four years and chooses Abu Bakr, Umar, and Utman as the next three caliphs. Ali finally becomes caliph, but his caliphate ends after five years, when an assassin splits his skull with a poisoned saber. Of Ali's two sons, Hassan will be poisoned and Hussein will fall in battle. The death of Ali's family deprives the Shiites of the chance to win power, which passes to the Sunni Omayyad, Abassid, and Ottoman dynasties. The caliphate, which Mohammed had conceived as a simple and modest institution, becomes a hereditary monarchy. In this situation the plebeian, pious, poverty-stricken Shiites, appalled by the nouveau-riche style of the victorious caliphs, go over to the opposition.

All this happens in the middle of the seventh century, but it has remained a living and passionately dwelt-on history to this day. When a devout Shiite talks about his faith he will constantly return to those remote histories and relate tearfully the massacre at Karbala in which Hussein had his head cut off. A skeptical, ironic European will think, God, what can any of that mean today? But if he expresses such thoughts aloud, he provokes the anger and hatred of the Shiite.

The Shiites have indeed had a tragic fate, and the sense of tragedy, of the historical wrongs and misfortunes that accompany them, is encoded deep within their consciousness. The world contains communities for whom nothing has gone right for centuries—everything has slipped through their hands, and every ray of hope has faded as soon as it began to shine—these people seem to bear some sort of fatal brand. So it is with the Shiites. For this reason, perhaps, they have an air of dead seriousness, of fervent unsettling adherence to their arguments and principles, and also (this is only an impression, of course) of sadness.

As soon as the Shiites (who constitute barely a tenth of all Muslims, the rest being Sunnis) go into opposition, the persecution begins. To this day they live the memory of the centuries of pogroms against them, and so they close themselves off in ghettoes, use signals only they understand, and devise conspiratorial forms of behavior. But the blows keep falling on their heads.

Gradually they start to look for safer places where they will have a better chance of survival. In those times of difficult and slow communication, in which distance and space constitute an efficient isolator, a separating wall, the Shiites try to move as far as possible from the center of power (which lies first in Damascus and later in Baghdad). They scatter throughout the world, across mountains and deserts, and descend step by step underground. So the Shiite diaspora, which has lasted till today, comes into being. The epic of the Shiites is full of acts of incredible abjuration, courage, and spiritual strength. A part of the wandering community heads east. Crossing the Tigris and the Euphrates, it passes through the mountains of Zagros and reaches the Iranian desert plateau.

At this time, Iran, exhausted and laid waste by centuries of war with Byzantium, has been conquered by Arabs who are spreading the new faith, Islam. This process is going on slowly, amid continual fighting. Until now the Iranians have had an official religion, Zoroastrianism, related to the ruling Sassanid dynasty. Now comes the attempt to impose upon them another official religion, associated with a new and, what's more, a foreign regime—Sunni Islam. It seems like jumping from the frying pan into the fire.

But exactly at this moment the poor, exhausted, wretched Shiites, still bearing the visible traces of the Gehenna they have lived through, appear. The Iranians discover that these Shiites are Muslims and, additionally (as they claim), the only legitimate Muslims, the only preservers of a pure faith for which they are ready to give their lives. Well, fine, say the Iranians—but what about your Arab brothers who have conquered us? Brothers? cry the outraged Shiites. Those Arabs are Sunnis, usurpers and our persecutors. They murdered Ali and seized power. No, we don't acknowledge them. We are in opposition! Having made this proclamation, the Shiites ask if they might rest after their long journey and request a jug of cold water.

This pronouncement by the barefoot newcomers sets the Iranians thinking along important lines. You can be a Muslim without being an establishment Muslim. What's more, you can be an opposition Muslim! And that makes you an even better Muslim! They feel empathy for these poor, wronged Shiites. At this moment the Iranians themselves are poor and feel wronged. They have been ruined by war, and an invader controls their country. So they quickly find a common language with these exiles who are looking for shelter and counting on their hospitality. The Iranians begin to listen to the Shiite preachers and finally accept their faith.

In this adroit maneuver one can see all the intelligence and independence of the Iranians. They have a particular talent for preserving their independence under conditions of subjugation. For hundreds of years the Iranians have been the victims of conquest, aggression, and partition. They have been ruled for centuries on end by foreigners or local regimes dependent on foreign powers, and yet they have preserved their culture and language, their impressive personality and so much spiritual fortitude that in propitious circumstances they can arise reborn from the ashes. During the twenty-five centuries of their recorded history the Iranians have always, sooner or later, managed to outwit anyone with the impudence to try ruling them. Sometimes they have to resort to the weapons of uprising and revolution to obtain their goal, and then they pay the tragic levy of blood. Sometimes they use the tactic of passive resistance, which they apply in a particularly consistent and radical way. When they get fed up with an authority that has become unbearable, the whole country freezes, the whole nation does a disappearing act. Authority gives orders but no one is listening, it frowns but no one is looking, it raises its voice but that voice is as one crying in the wilderness. Then authority falls apart like a house of cards. The most common Iranian technique, however, is absorption, active assimilation, in a way that turns the foreign sword into the Iranians' own weapon.

And so it is after the Arab conquest. You want Islam, they tell the conquerors, so Islam you'll get—but in our own national form and in an independent, rebellious version. It will be faith, but an Iranian faith that expresses our spirit, our culture, and our independence. This philosophy underlies the Iranian decision to accept Islam. They accept it in the Shiite variant, which at that time is the faith of the wronged and the conquered, an instrument of contestation and resistance, the ideology of the unhumbled who are ready to suffer but will not renounce their principles because they want to preserve their distinctness and dignity. Shiism will become not

71

only the national religion of the Iranians but also their refuge and shelter, a form of national survival and, at the right moments, of struggle and liberation.

Iran transforms itself into the most restless province of the Muslim empire. Someone is always plotting here, there is always some uprising, masked messengers appear and disappear, secret leaflets and brochures circulate. The representatives of the occupying authorities, the Arab governors, spread terror and end up with results opposite to what they'd intended. In answer to the official terror the Iranian Shiites begin to fight back, but not in a frontal assault, for which they are too weak. An element of the Shiite community from now on will be— if one can use such a term—the terrorist fringe. Down to the present day, small, conspiratorial terrorist organizations that know neither fear nor pity operate in Iran. Half of the killings blamed on the ayatollahs are performed on the sentences of these groups. Generally, history regards the Shiites as the founders of the theory and practice of individual terror as a means of combat.

Fervor, orthodoxy, and an obsessive, fanatic concern for doctrinal purity characterize the Shiites as they characterize every group that is persecuted, condemned to the ghetto, and made to fight for its survival. A persecuted man cannot survive without an unshakeable faith in the correctness of his choice. He must protect the values that led him to that choice. Thus, all the schisms—and Shiism has lived through dozens of them— had one thing in common: They were all, as we would put it, ultra-leftist. A fanatical branch was always springing up to accuse the remainder of its co-religionists of atrophied zeal, of treating lightly the dictates of faith, of expediency and taking the easy way out. Once the split took place the most fervid of the schismatics would take up arms to finish off the enemies of Islam, redeeming in blood (because they themselves often perished) the treachery and laziness of their backsliding brothers.

The Iranian Shiites have been living underground, in the catacombs, for eight hundred years. Their life recalls the suffering and trials of the first Christians. Sometimes it seems that they will be extirpated completely, that a final annihilation awaits them. For years they have been taking refuge in the mountains, holing up in caves, dying of hunger. Their songs that survive from these years, full of rue and despair, prophesy the end of the world.

But there have also been calmer periods, and then Iran became the refuge of all the oppositionists in the Muslim empire, who arrive from all corners of the world to find shelter, encouragement, and support among the plotting Shiites. They could also take lessons in the great Shiite school of conspiracy. They might, for example, master the principle of dissembling *(taqija),* which facilitates survival. This principle allows the Shiite, when he finds himself up against a stronger opponent, seemingly to accept the prevailing religion and acclaim himself a believer as long as doing so will save him and his people. Shiism also teaches *kitman,* the art of disorienting one's enemies, which allows the Shiite to contradict his own assurances and pretend that he is an idiot when danger threatens. Iran thus becomes a medieval mecca of malcontents, rebels, strange varieties of hermits, prophets, ecstatics, shady heretics, stigmatics, mystics, and fortunetellers, who pour in along every road to teach, contemplate, pray, and soothsay. All this creates the atmosphere of religiosity, exaltation, and mysticism so characteristic of the country. I was very devout in school, says an Iranian, and all the kids thought I had a radiant halo around my head. Try imagining a European leader who writes that once when he was out riding he fell over a cliff and would have died except that a saint reached out a hand to save him. Yet the last Shah described such a scene in a book of his and all Iran read it seriously. Superstitious beliefs, such as faith in numbers, omens, symbols, prophecies, and revelations, have deep roots here.

In the sixteenth century the rulers of the Safavid dynasty raised Shiism to the dignity of official religion. What had been the ideology of mass opposition became the ideology of a state in opposition—for the Iranian state opposed the Sunni domination of the Ottoman Empire. But with time the relations between the monarchy and Shiism grew worse and worse.

The point is that Shiites not only reject the authority of the caliphs; they barely tolerate any lay authority at all. Iran constitutes the unique case of a country whose people believe only in the reign of their religious leaders, the imams, one of whom, the last, left this world (according to rational, if not to Shiite, criteria) in the ninth century.

Here we reach the essence of Shiite doctrine, the main act of faith for its believers. Deprived of any chance to win the caliphate, the Shiites turn their backs on the caliphs and henceforth acknowledge only the leaders of their own faith, the imams. Ali is the first imam, Hassan and Hussein his sons the second and third, and so on until the twelfth. All these imams died violent deaths at the hands of caliphs who saw them as dangerous rivals. The Shiites believe, however, that the twelfth and last imam, Mohammed, did not perish but disappeared into the cave under the great mosque at Samarra, in Iraq. This happened in 878. He is the Hidden Imam, the Awaited One, who will appear at the appropriate time as Mahdi (The One Led By God) to establish the kingdon of righteousness on earth. Afterward comes the end of the world. The Shiites believe that if the Twelfth Imam were not a living presence, the world would cease to be. They draw their spiritual strength from their faith in the Awaited One, they live and die for that faith. This is the simple human longing of a wronged, suffering community that finds hope and, above all, its sense of life, in that idea. We do not know when that Awaited One will appear; it could happen at any moment, even today. Then the tears will cease and each will take his seat at the table of plenty.

The Awaited One is the only leader the Shiites are willing to submit themselves to totally. To a lesser degree they acknowledge their religious helmsmen, the ayatollahs, and to a still lesser degree, the Shah. Because the Awaited One is the Adored, the focus of a cult, the Shah can be at best the Tolerated One.

From the time of the Safavids a dual authority, of the monarchy and the mosque, has existed in Iran. The relations between these two forces have varied but have never been overly friendly. If something disturbs this balance of forces, however, if, as happened, the Shah tries to impose total authority (with, to boot, the help of foreign backers), then the people gather in the mosques and the fighting starts.

For Shiites, the mosque is far more than a place of worship. It is also a haven where they can weather a storm and even save their lives. It is a territory protected by immunity, where authority has no right to enter. It used to be the custom that if a rebel pursued by the police took refuge in a mosque, he was safe and could not be removed by force.

There are marked differences in the construction of a mosque and a Christian church. A church is a closed space, a place of prayer, meditation, and silence. If someone starts talking, others rebuke him. A mosque is different. Its largest component is an open courtyard where people can pray, walk, discuss, even hold meetings. An exuberant social and political life goes on there. The Iranian who has been harassed at work, who encounters only grumpy bureaucrats looking for bribes, who is everywhere spied on by the police, comes to the mosque to find balance and calm, to recover his dignity. Here no one hurries him or calls him names. Hierarchies disappear, all are equal, all are brothers, and—because the mosque is also a place of conversation and dialogue—a man can speak his mind, grumble, and listen to what others have to say. What a relief it is, how much everyone needs it. This is why, as the dictatorship turns the screws and an ever more oppressive silence clouds the streets and workplaces, the mosque fills more and more with people and the hum of voices. Not all those who come here are fervent Muslims, not all are drawn by a sudden wave of devotion—they come because they want to breathe, because they want to feel like people. Even Savak has limited freedom of action on the grounds of the mosque. Nevertheless, the police arrest and torture many clerics who speak out against the abuse of power. Ayatollah Saidi dies during torture, on "the frying pan." Ayatollah Azarshari dies soon afterward, when Savak agents throw him into a pot of boiling oil. Ayatollah Teleghani emerges from prison with only a short time to live because of the way he has been treated. He has no eyelids. As he watched, Savak agents raped Teleghani's daughter, and when the ayatollah closed his eyes, they burned his eyelids with cigarettes so he would have to watch. All this goes on in the 1970s. But in his policy toward the mosque, the Shah entangles himself in no small web of contradictions. On the one hand he persecutes the clerical opposition and, on the other—always courting public favor—he declares himself a fervent Muslim, perpetually makes pilgrimages to the holy places, immerses himself in prayer, and solicits the blessing of the mullahs. How, then, can he declare open war on the mosques?

The Shiite also visits the mosque because it is always close, in the neighborhood, on the way to everywhere. Teheran contains a thousand mosques. The tourist's uninstructed eye spots only a few of the most impressive ones. But the majority of them, especially in the poorer neighborhoods, are modest buildings difficult to distinguish from the flimsily constructed little houses in which the underclass lives. Built of the same clay, they melt into the monotonous faces of the lanes, back alleys, and street corners, resulting in a working, intimate climate between the Shiite and his mosque. No need to make long treks, no need to get dressed up: The mosque is everyday life, life itself.

The first Shiites to reach Iran were city people, small merchants and craftsmen. They would enclose themselves in their ghettoes, build mosques, and set up their market stands and little shops next door. Craftsmen opened workshops nearby. Because Muslims should wash before they pray, baths appeared as well. And because a Muslim likes to drink tea or coffee and have a bite to eat after praying, there were also restaurants and coffee shops close at hand. Thus comes into being that phenomenon of the Iranian cityscape, the bazaar—a colorful, crowded, noisy mystical-commercial-gustatory nexus. If someone says, "I'm going to the bazaar," he does not necessarily mean that he needs his shopping bag. You go to the bazaar to pray, to meet friends, to do business, to sit in a café. You can go there to catch up on gossip and take part in an opposition rally. Without having to run all over town, the Shiite finds in one place, the bazaar, all that is indispensable for earthly existence and, through prayer and offerings, also ensures his eternal life.

From the Notes

Mahmud Azari returned to Iran at the beginning of 1977. He had lived in London for eight years, supporting himself by translating books for various publishers and writing copy for advertising agencies. He was an older, solitary man who liked to spend his leisure time walking and talking with his compatriots. During such meetings the conversation centered around purely English problems; Savak was ubiquitous, even in London, and wise people avoided talking about the problems of their homeland.

Near the end of his sojourn he received several letters, through private channels, from his brother in Teheran. The brother wrote that interesting times were coming and urged him to return. Mahmud feared interesting times, but since his brother had always held the ascendancy in their family, he packed his luggage and returned to Teheran.

He couldn't recognize the city.

The onetime desert oasis had become a stunning overcrowded metropolis of five million people. A million cars strained in the narrow streets, immobile because a line going one way would meet a line going another way, while other lines of traffic were cutting across, slicing through from left and right, from northeast and southwest, forming giant smoking, roaring, stellar coils stuck in narrow cagelike lanes. Thousands of car horns blared from dawn to dusk, without purpose.

He noticed that the people, once quiet and courteous, now quarreled at the slightest provocation, burst out angrily for no reason at all, jumped down each other's throats, screamed and cursed. These people seemed like weird, surrealistic bifurcated monsters whose upper half would bow obsequiously before anyone important or endowed with authority, while at the same time their hind parts were trampling on anyone weaker. This apparently led to an inner equilibrium that, however mean and pitiable, made it possible for them to survive.

He found himself dreading the thought that, when he came face to face with such a monster, he would be unable to tell which of its functions, the bowing or the trampling, would come first. But he found soon enough that the trampling reflex predominated; it naturally presented itself and withdrew only under the extreme pressure of grave circumstances.

During his first days he went to the local park, sat down beside a man on a bench, and tried to start a conversation. But the man stood up without a word and walked briskly away. After a time, he approached another passer-by, who gave him a look of terror as if he had run into a lunatic. So he gave up and decided to return to his hotel.

The gruff, petulant man at the desk told him he had

to report to the police. For the first time in eight years he felt true terror and realized instantly that such terror can never be outgrown: It was the same touch of ice against the bare back, the same heaviness in his feet that he remembered so well from years gone by.

The police occupied an obscure, foul-smelling building down the street from the hotel. Mahmud took his place in a long line of sullen, listless people. On the other side of the railing, the policemen were sitting reading newspapers. Total silence reigned in the big, crowded room: The police were reading, and no one in the line dared so much as whisper. Then, the station suddenly opened for business. The police scraped their chairs back and forth, rummaged through their desks, and began cursing their waiting clients with the choicest obscenities.

Where does this universal boorishness come from? wondered the frightened Mahmud. When his turn came, the police gave him a questionnaire and told him to fill it out immediately. He kept hesitating over each item and noticed that the whole room was watching him suspiciously. Terrified, he began writing nervously and awkwardly as if he were semi-illiterate. He felt sweat breaking out on his forehead, discovered he had forgotten his handkerchief, and began perspiring all the more.

After handing in the questionnaire he hurried out into the street and, walking along distractedly, ran into another pedestrian. The stranger started cursing him. Some passers-by stopped to gawk and in this way Mahmud committed a crime—his behavior had provoked a gathering. The law forbade all unauthorized assemblies. A policeman showed up and Mahmud had to explain that it was all an accident and that not a word had been spoken against the Shah during the whole contretemps.

Nevertheless the policeman took down his name and address and pocketed a thousand rials.

Mahmud returned downcast to the hotel. The police had already written his name down—twice, in fact. He started thinking about what would happen if the two entries were brought together somehow. Then he consoled himself with the thought that it might all vanish in the bureaucracy's bottomless confusion.

His brother came by in the morning and Mahmud told him, as soon as they had greeted each other, that the police already had his name twice. Wouldn't it be wiser, he asked, to go back to London?

Mahmud's brother wanted to talk, but he pointed to the light fixture, telephone, electrical outlets, and night lamp; let's take a ride in the suburbs, he said. In the brother's old, beat-up car they headed for the mountains. When the road grew deserted they parked. It was March, with a keen wind and snow piled all around. They hid behind a tall boulder and stood there shivering.

("It was then that my brother told me I had to stay because the revolution had begun and I would be needed. 'What revolution? Are you mad?' I asked. All disturbances frightened me, and in general I can't stand politics. Every day I practice yoga, read poetry, and translate. What do I need politics for? But my brother told me I didn't understand anything and proceeded to explain. The starting point, he said, was Washington. That was where our fate would be decided. 'Right now, Jimmy Carter is talking about human rights. The Shah will have to pay attention. He has to stop using torture, release some prisoners, and create at least the appearance of democracy. That will be enough to get us started!' My brother was becoming excited, and I hushed him even though there was no one around. During this meeting he handed me a typescript of more than two hundred pages. It was a memorandum by the writer Ali Asqara Jawadi—an open letter to the Shah. In it, Jawadi wrote about the current crisis, about the subjugation of the country, and the scandals of the monarchy. My brother said that the document was circulating secretly and that people were making more copies of it. 'Now,' he added, 'we are waiting to see how the Shah responds. Whether Jawadi goes to jail or not. For the time being he is getting threatening telephone calls but nothing more. There is a café he comes to—you'll be able to talk to him.' I replied I was afraid to meet someone who was surely under surveillance.")

They went back to the city, where Mahmud locked himself in his room and spent the night reading the memorandum. Jawadi accused the Shah of destroying the moral foundations of the country. All thinking, he wrote, was being annihilated, and the most enlightened people were being silenced. Culture found itself behind bars or had to go underground. Jawadi warned that you could not measure progress by the number of tanks and machines. Man, with his sense of liberty and dignity, was the measure of progress. As he read, Mahmud listened for footsteps in the corridor.

The next day he worried about what to do with the typescript. Not wanting to leave it in his room, he took it with him. But as he walked down the street he realized that such a bundle of paper looked suspicious, so he bought a newspaper, which he folded around the typescript. Even so, he was in constant fear of being stopped and searched. It was the worst in the hotel lobby, where he was certain the package attracted attention. So he decided to limit his comings and goings, just to be on the safe side.

Mahmud tried gradually to find out what had happened to his old friends, his university classmates. Some, unfortunately, had died, many had emigrated, and a few were in jail. At last, though, he managed to track down several current addresses. At the university he called on Ali Kaidi, an old companion on mountain excursions. Kaidi had become a professor of botany, a specialist in sclerophyllous plants. Cautiously, Mahmud asked him about the situation in the country. Kaidi thought for a moment and said that for years he had devoted all his time to sclerophyllous plants. He went on to develop the topic, saying that sclerophyllous plants were to be found in areas with specific climatic conditions: rain in winter, summers hot and dry. In winter, it was ephemeral species like the therophytes and geophytes that flourished, while in summer it was the xerophytes, which had the ability to limit their transpiration. Mahmud, to whom these words meant nothing, asked his friend in a general way whether major events could be expected. Kaidi again fell to musing and began after a while to talk about the splendid crown of the Atlantic cedar (*Cedrus atlanticus*). "And yet," he added, warming to the subject, "I have examined the Himalayan cedar (*Cedrus deodora*), which grows in our country, and I must say that it is even more beautiful!"

Another day he came across an old friend with whom he had tried to write a play at school. Now this friend had become mayor of Karaj. The mayor invited Mahmud to dinner at a good restaurant, and near the end of the meal the latter asked about the mood of society. The mayor did not want to go beyond the affairs of his town. In Karaj, he said, they were asphalting the main roads. They had begun to build a sewer system, which even Teheran lacked. The crushing avalanche of numbers and jargon convinced Mahmud he had asked the wrong question. But he made up his mind to press on and inquired of his old schoolmate what was the most common subject of conversation in his city. "How should I know? Their own problems. These people don't think. Nothing matters to them. They are lazy, apolitical, and they can't see past the ends of their noses. The problems of Iran, indeed! What do they care?" And he went on talking about how they had built a new paraldehyde factory and were going to cover the country with their paraldehyde. Mahmud felt like an ignoramus, a relic, because he didn't even know what the word meant. "And, generally speaking," he asked his friend, "don't you have any bigger problems to worry about?" The other man replied, "And how!" He leaned over the table and whispered, "The output of these new factories is only fit to be thrown away. Trash and scrap. People don't want to work, and they don't give a damn about what they produce. Everywhere there's the same listlessness, some kind of vague, sullen resistance. The whole country is stuck on a sandbar." "But why?" Mahmud demanded. "I can't say," his friend answered, sitting up and beckoning to the waiter. "It's hard for me to say"—and Mahmud watched as the frank soul of the sometime schoolboy dramatist, having emerged for a moment to voice some unusual words, swiftly disappeared again behind a barricade of generators, conveyors, relays, and control keys.

("For these people the concrete has become an asylum, a hideout, salvation. Cedar—well, yes, that's something concrete; so is asphalt. You can speak out about the concrete, express yourself as freely as you like. The great thing about the concrete is that it has its own clearly demarcated armed frontiers with warning bells along them. When a mind immersed in the concrete begins to approach that border, the bells warn that just beyond lies the field of treacherous general ideas, undesirable reflections, and syntheses. At the sound of this signal the cautious mind recoils and dives back into the concrete. We can see the whole process in the face of our interlocutor. He might be going along, talking in the most lively of ways, quoting numbers, percentages, names, and dates. We can see how firmly he's anchored in the concrete, like a rider in the saddle. Then we ask: 'That's all well and good, but why are people, in some way, shall we say, imperfectly satisfied?' At this point we can see how his face changes. The alarm bells have gone off: *Attention! You are about to cross the border of the concrete!* He grows silent and looks desperately for a way out—which is, of course, to retreat back into the concrete. Glad to have escaped the trap, panting with relief, he again starts talking with animation, haranguing and crushing us with the concrete in any form whatsoever: an object, an existence, a creature, or a phenomenon. It is a characteristic of disparate concretes that they cannot join together spontaneously to create general images. For example, two negative concretes can exist side by side, but they will not form a joint image until human thought welds them together. But the alarm bells prevent that synthesizing thought from ever occurring, so the negative concretes go on coexisting without forming any disturbing pattern. To succeed in making each person close himself within the borders of his concrete existence is to create an atomized society made up of n-number of concrete individuals unable to unite into a harmoniously acting comity.")

Mahmud, however, decided to tear himself away from

mundane problems and sail into the realm of imagination and emotion. He traced another friend who, he learned, had become a respected poet. Hassan Rezvani received him in a luxurious modern villa. They sat at the edge of the swimming pool (the summer heat had set in) sipping gin and tonic from frosty glasses. Hassan complained of tiredness: He had just returned the day before from a trip to Montreal, Chicago, Paris, Geneva, and Athens. He had traveled around giving lectures on the Great Civilization, the Revolution of the Shah and the Nation. It had been hard work, he confessed, because noisy subversives had prevented him from speaking and had insulted him. Hassan showed Mahmud a new volume of his poems, dedicated to the Shah. The first poem bore the title "Where He Casts His Glance, Flowers Bloom." If, so the poem said, the Shah merely looked anywhere at all, a carnation or a tulip would blossom forth.

> And where longer his glance reposes,
> There blossom roses.

Another poem was titled "Where He Stands, a Spring Appears." In these verses the author assured his readers that wherever the monarch sets his foot, a spring of crystal-clear water will appear:

> Let the Shah stop somewhere and stand
> And a broad river flows across the land.

These verses were read on the radio and in schools. The monarch himself referred to them in flattering terms and endowed Hassan with a Pahlavi Foundation fellowship.

Walking down the street one day, Mahmud saw a man standing under a tree. Drawing nearer, with difficulty he recognized Mohsen Jalaver, with whom he had broken into print years before in a student magazine. Mahmud knew that Mohsen had been tortured and jailed for sheltering a mujahedeen friend in his apartment. Mahmud stopped and held out his hand in greeting. Mohsen looked at him blankly. Mahmud pronounced his own name as a reminder. Mohsen reacted only by saying, "I don't care." He just stood there, slumped over and staring at the ground. "Let's go somewhere," Mahmud said. "I'd like to talk with you." Still motionless, his head drooping, Mohsen replied, "I don't care." Mahmud felt a chill. "Look," he tried again, "why don't we make a date to talk soon?" Mohsen didn't reply, but only slumped lower. Finally, in a strangled whisper, he said, "Take the rats away."

Sometime later, Mahmud rented a small apartment in the center of town. He was still unpacking when three men came in, greeted him as a new resident of the district, and asked whether he belonged to Rastakhiz, the Shah's party. Mahmud said he did not belong, since he had only recently returned from spending some years in Europe. This raised their suspicions: Those who had a chance to leave seldom returned. They began asking why he had come back, and one of them wrote down Mahmud's answers in a notebook. With terror, Mahmud realized he was now going into the records for the third time. When the visitors handed him a membership application, Mahmud replied that he had been apolitical all his life and did not intend to join. They looked at him dumfounded—the new tenant, they must have thought, could not know what he was saying. So they gave him a leaflet in which a statement of the Shah's was printed

in capital letters: THOSE WHO WILL NOT JOIN THE RAS-
TAKHIZ PARTY ARE EITHER TRAITORS WHO BELONG IN
PRISON OR PEOPLE WHO DO NOT BELIEVE IN THE SHAH,
THE NATION, AND THE HOMELAND AND THUS OUGHT NOT
TO EXPECT TO BE TREATED IN THE SAME WAY AS OTH-
ERS. Nevertheless, Mahmud had the backbone to ask to
think it over for a day, saying that he wanted to discuss
it with his brother.

"You have no choice," his brother said. "We all belong! The whole nation has to belong as if it were a single man." Mahmud went home, and when the activists
returned the next day he declared his allegiance to the
party. Thus he became a warrior of the Great Civilization.

Soon he received an invitation to the nearby Rastakhiz local headquarters. A meeting of party members in
the creative arts was in progress, attended by all those
who wanted to contribute their work to the thirty-seventh
anniversary of the Shah's coronation. The whole life of
the empire flowed from anniversary to anniversary in an
unctuous, ornate, dignified rhythm with the solemn and
resplendent celebration of each date connected to the
Shah and his outstanding achievements: the White
Revolution and the Great Civilization. Vast staffs of people kept watch, calendars in hand, to make sure the
monarch's birthday, his last wedding, his coronation, and
the births of the heir to the throne and the other hap-
pily begotten offspring would not be forgotten. New feasts
swelled the list of traditional holidays. As soon as one
celebration ended, the preparations for the next one began, fever and excitement charged the air, all work came
to a halt, and everyone made ready for the next day that
would pass amid sumptuous banqueting, showers of
distinctions, and a sublime liturgy.

As Mahmud was leaving the meeting, the writer and translator Golam Qasemi came up to him. They had not seen each other for years; while Mahmud was staying in London, Golam had remained at home writing stories that glorified the Great Civilization. He lived a splendid life, with free access to the palace and his books published in leather bindings. Golam had something to tell Mahmud. He dragged him to an Armenian café, spread a weekly on the table, and said proudly, "Look what I've managed to get published!" It was his translation of a poem by Paul Eluard. Mahmud glanced at it and said, "Well, what's so remarkable about this? What are you so proud of?" "What?" Golam burst out. "Don't you understand anything? Read it carefully:

Now is the time of sorrow, of darkest night
When even the blind must not be sent outside."

As he read, he underlined every word with his fingernail. "All the effort, all the trouble it took me," he said excitedly, "to get this printed, to convince Savak that it could appear! In this country where everything is supposed to inspire optimism, blossoming, smiles—suddenly 'the time of sorrow'! Can you imagine?" Golam was wearing the face of the victor, elated at his own courage.

It was only at this moment, looking at Golam's cunning face, that Mahmud believed for the first time in the approaching revolution. It seemed to him that he suddenly understood everything. Golam can sense the coming catastrophe. He is beginning to maneuver shrewdly, to shift his battle lines, to try to purge himself of blame, to pay tribute to the rumbling force that already resounds in his frightened and besieged heart. Golam has just sneaked a thumbtack onto the scarlet cushion the Shah sits on. This is hardly a bomb. It won't kill the Shah, but it makes Golam feel better—he has joined the opposition, however hermetically. Now he will show off the thumbtack, talk it up, seek the praise and recognition of his friends, and revel in the feeling of having shown his independence.

But Mahmud's old doubts come back in the evening. He and his brother were walking along streets that grew more and more empty, past faces deprived of any vitality. Exhausted pedestrians were trudging home or standing silently at bus stops. Some men were sitting against a wall, dozing, their faces on their knees. Mahmud pointed at them and asked, "Who is going to carry out this revolution of yours? They are all sleeping." His brother replied, "These very people will do it. One day they will sprout wings." But Mahmud could not imagine it.

("And yet early in the summer I myself began to feel something changing, something reviving in people, something in the air. The atmosphere was indefinable, a little like the first glimmer of consciousness after a tormenting dream. In the first place, the Americans forced the Shah to release some intellectuals from prison. The Shah cheated—he released some and locked up others. But the important thing was that he'd given in, and the first crack, the first little gap, appeared in the rigid system. Into that gap stepped people who wanted to resurrect the Iranian Writers' Organization, which the Shah had dissolved in '69. All organizations, even the most innocent, had been banned. Only Rastakhiz and the mosque remained. *Tertium non datur*. The government continued to say no to a writers' union. Accordingly, secret meetings began in private homes, most often in old country houses outside Teheran where it was easier to maintain secrecy. They called these meetings 'cultural evenings.' First there would be a poetry reading, and then the discussion of the current situation would begin. It was at one of these meetings that I first saw people who had been in prison. They were writers, scientists, and students. I looked closely at their faces, trying to see what scars great fear and suffering made. I thought they were behaving abnormally. They acted hesitantly, as if the light and the presence of others made them dizzy. They kept a watchful distance from their surroundings, as if the approach of any other person could lead to a beating. One of them looked awful—he had burn scars on his face and hands, and he walked with a cane. He was a student in the law school, and fedayeen brochures had been found in a search of his home. I remember his telling how he was led by the Savak agents into a big room, one of whose walls was white-hot iron. There were rails on the floor, a metal chair on the rails; the Savak men strapped him into the chair. Then they pushed a button and the chair began moving toward the wall in a slow, jerky movement, an inch a minute. He calculated it would take two hours to reach the wall, but after an hour he could no longer stand the heat and began shouting that he would admit everything, even though there was nothing to admit—he'd found the brochures lying in the street. We all listened silently as the student cried. I'll always remember what he then said: 'God,' he said, 'why have you chastised me with such a terrible deformity as thinking? Why have you taught me to think, instead of teaching me the humility of cattle!' In the end he fainted, and we carried him into the next room. Other survivors of the dungeon, in contrast, usually remained silent.")

But Savak quickly tracked down the location of these

meetings. One night, when they had left the house and were walking along the path by the road, Mahmud heard a sudden rustling in the bushes off to the side. After a moment of confusion he heard shouts. Then he felt a monstrous blow to the back of his head, and the darkness grew violently deeper. He staggered, fell face-first on the stone pathway, and lost consciousness. He came to in his brother's arms. In the darkness, his eyes swollen and covered with blood, he could barely make out his brother's gray, bruised face. He heard moans, someone cried out for help, and after a moment he recognized the voice of the student, who must have gone into shock. As if it came from deep in the earth, the voice kept repeating, "Why did you teach me to think? Why did you chastise me with this horrible deformity?" Now Mahmud could see that the arm of one of those standing near him was dangling, broken, and he saw another man kneeling by him with blood oozing from his mouth. Trying to keep close together, the group moved slowly toward the highway in deadly fear the beating would start again.

Next morning Mahmud stayed in bed with a swollen head and a stitched-up forehead. The housekeeper brought him a newspaper which had an account of the previous night's incident: "Last night in the vicinity of Kan, a group of recidivistic social outcasts organized a repugnant orgy at one of the local farmhouses. The patriotic inhabitants of the area complained several times about the impropriety and repulsiveness of their behavior. Nevertheless the riotous gang, instead of paying due attention to the local patriots, attacked them with stones and clubs. The people who were attacked had to defend themselves and restore order to the area." Mahmud groaned, feeling feverish, his head spinning.

"The Shah's days are numbered," Mahmud's brother was saying firmly a few days later. "No one can butcher a defenseless nation for years." "Numbered?" Mahmud asked in astonishment, lifting his bandaged head. "Have you lost your mind? Have you seen his army?" Of course his brother had seen it, the question was rhetorical. Mahmud had been constantly exposed to the imperial divisions at the movies and on television: parades, maneuvers, fighters, rockets, the barrels of heavy artillery aiming straight at his heart. He'd look with disgust at the rows of elderly generals who drew themselves laboriously to attention before the monarch. I wonder, he'd think, how they'd behave if a real bomb went off nearby. They'd all have heart attacks. Every month more and more tanks and mortars crowded the TV screen. Mahmud thought they constituted a terrible force that could grind any opposition into dust and blood.

The scorching summer months began. The desert that embraces Teheran from the south panted fire. Mahmud felt better now and decided to resume his habit of evening walks after a long hiatus. He strolled out. It was late. He was walking through dark little streets near some grim, gigantic construction site being rapidly completed—the new Rastakhiz headquarters. He thought he saw a figure moving in the darkness and heard someone coming out of the bushes. But there are no bushes here! He tried to calm down. Frightened, nevertheless, he turned into the next street. He was afraid, even though he knew the fear had no precise cause. He felt cold and decided to head home. He was walking downhill near the center of town. Suddenly he heard footsteps behind him. He was surprised, because he had been sure the street was empty, that there was no one around. He quickened his pace involuntarily, and whoever was behind him did the same. They walked in step for a while, rhythmically, like two honor guards. Mahmud decided to speed up even more. Now he was walking with short, sharp steps. The other one did the same, and came even closer. Mahmud, trying to think of a way out, slowed down. But fear conquered common sense, and he lengthened his stride again to escape. He was covered with goose pimples. He was terrified of provoking the other. He thought he was postponing the blow, but whoever was behind him drew closer and Mahmud could hear the other's breathing as their steps echoed together in the tunnel of the street. Finally Mahmud broke down and started to run. The other gave chase and Mahmud rushed onward, his jacket flapping like a black banner. Suddenly he realized others had joined the pursuit, dozens of footsteps were rumbling behind him with the clatter of an incipient avalanche. He kept running though he was out of breath. He was soaking wet, semiconscious, and felt he would collapse in a second. With the last of his strength he grabbed hold of a nearby gate, swung himself up onto the grating of a barred window, and hung there, suspended. He thought his heart would burst, and he felt an alien fist breaking through his ribs dealing painful, deathly blows ravaging his insides. Finally he brought himself under control and looked around. The only living soul in the street was a gray cat hurrying along the wall. Slowly, with his hand over his heart, he dragged himself home, broken, depressed, vanquished.

("It all began with that night attack when we were leaving the meeting. From then on I felt the fear. It would hit me at the most unexpected moments. I was ashamed, but I couldn't deal with it. It began to disturb me profoundly. I thought with horror that by carrying that fear inside I'd involuntarily become part of a system founded on fear. A terrible, yet indissoluble, relation, a sort of pathological symbiosis, had established itself between me and the dictator. Through my fear I was supporting a system I hated. The Shah could depend on me—on my fear, that is, on the fact that my fear would not let him down. If I could have gotten rid of my fear, I could have undermined the foundations of the throne just a little, but I was as yet unable to do that.")

Mahmud felt bad all summer. Apathetically he would receive news his brother brought him.

Everyone was living on top of a volcano in those days, and anything could set off the eruption. A horse ran mad and attacked people in Kermanshah—a peasant had ridden the animal into town and tethered it to a tree along the main street. It shied and reared up at some passing cars, broke free, and injured several people. Finally a soldier shot it. People crowded around the dead animal. The police arrived and began to disperse the crowd. Someone shouted, "And where were the police when the horse was trampling the people?" Then a fight broke out. The police opened fire. But the crowd kept growing. The crowd was boiling mad, and people began putting up barricades. Then the army came in and the town commander ordered a curfew. Mahmud's brother asked him, "Do you think it would have taken much more for an uprising to erupt there?" But Mahmud, as usual, thought his brother was exaggerating.

As Mahmud was walking along Reza Khan Boulevard one day early in September, he noticed a commotion in the street. He could see, in the distance, at the main entrance to the university, military trucks, helmets, guns, and soldiers in green fatigues. They were grabbing students and hauling them off to the trucks. Mahmud heard screams and saw young men running away down the street. Suddenly there was a wail of sirens, and the trucks full of students began moving up the street. The students stood squeezed onto the platforms, their hands bound with ropes, soldiers surrounding them. Apparently the roundup was over, and Mahmud decided to go tell his brother the army had raided the university. A young high school teacher named Ferejdun Ganji, whom Mahmud remembered meeting at the cultural evening before the police assault, was there. According to Mahmud's brother, when Ganji had gone to school the day after the night assault, the principal, who had already received a telephone call from Savak, fired him, shouting that he was a hooligan and a bully and that he, the principal, was ashamed to let innocent students see him. Ganji had now been unemployed for a long time, roaming around in search of work.

The brother decided they'd go to dinner at the bazaar. In the crowded stuffy back alleys, Mahmud noticed a lot of young people staggering around in an opium daze. Some of them were sitting on the sidewalk, staring ahead with glassy, unseeing eyes. Others were harassing passers-by, calling them names and making fists at them. "How can the police tolerate this?" he asked his brother. "Quite easily," the latter answered. "From time to time a crowd like this comes in handy. Today they'll be given clubs and a few pennies and sent to beat up the students. Later the press will write about the healthy, patriotic youth who answered the call of the party and taught a lesson to the good-for-nothing dregs of society nesting within the university's walls."

They entered a restaurant and took a table in the middle of the room. They were still waiting for service when Mahmud noticed two brawny men lounging at the next table. Savak!—the idea shot through his mind. "What do you say?" he asked his brother and Ganji. "Let's move closer to the door." They changed tables, and the waiter appeared at once. But while his brother was ordering, Mahmud's eye fell on two handsome, coquettishly dressed men holding hands. Savak agents pretending to be homosexuals! he thought with terror. "I'd rather sit by the window," he suggested to his brother. "I want to see what's going on in the bazaar." They moved to the new table. Barely had they begun to eat, however, when three men came in and, without a word, as if they had planned it in advance, took a table at the same window from which Mahmud was observing the bazaar. "We're being watched," he whispered, and at the same instant he noticed that the waiters, who had been following their table hopping, were looking at them suspiciously. He realized that, to the waiters, they themselves must have looked like Savak agents moving around the room in search of prey. He lost his appetite and the food swelled in his mouth. Pushing his plate aside, he motioned with his head to leave.

They reached his brother's home and decided to drive to the mountains to get away from the wearying city and breathe some fresh air. They drove north through the nouveau-riche district of Shemiran, where the air still smelled of cement. They passed imposing mansions, ostentatious villas, luxurious restaurants and dress shops, spacious gardens, exclusive country clubs with swimming pools and tennis courts. Here every square foot of desert—the desert stretched away in all directions—cost hundreds if not thousands of dollars and even so was in great demand. This was the charmed circle of the court elite, another world, another planet.

In the next weeks, there were new demonstrations, new protest letters, and secret lectures and discussions. In November a committee for the defense of human rights and an underground students' union were established. At times Mahmud visited the nearby mosques and saw the crowds of people there, but the prevailing attitude of fervent piety remained alien to him, and he did not know how to make contact with that world. You have to ask yourself, he thought, where all these people are going. Most of them could not even read and write. They found themselves in an incomprehensible, hostile world that was cheating and exploiting them and held them in contempt. They wanted to find some sort of shelter for themselves, some relief and protection. But one thing they knew: In this unfriendly reality, only Allah remained the same as back in their villages, as always, as everywhere.

He was reading a lot now and translating London and Kipling. When he remembered his English years, he thought about the differences between Europe and Asia and repeated Kipling's formula to himself: "East is east, and West is west, and never . . ." Never, no, they will never meet, and they will never understand each other. Asia will reject every European transplant as a foreign body. The Europeans will be shocked and outraged, but they will be unable to change Asia. In Europe epochs succeed each other, the new drives out the old, the earth periodically cleanses itself of its past so that people of our century have trouble understanding our ancestors. Here it is different, here the past is as alive as the present, the unpredictable cruel Stone Age coexists with the calculating, cool age of electronics—the two eras live in the same man, who is as much the descendant of

Genghis Khan as he is the student of Edison . . . if, that is, he ever comes into contact with Edison's world.

One night at the beginning of January Mahmud heard a banging on his door. He jumped out of bed.

("It was my brother. I could see he was extremely agitated. Out in the corridor, he said only one word— 'Massacre!' He didn't want to sit down, kept walking around the room, spoke chaotically. He said the police had opened fire on civilians in the streets of Qom. He mentioned five hundred dead. A lot of women and children had perished. It had all come about because of what seemed like a trivial matter. An article criticizing Khomeini had appeared in the newspaper *Etelat*. It had been written by someone from the palace or the government. When the paper reached Qom, Khomeini's city, people started gathering in the streets to talk about it. The police opened fire. A panic broke out in the square— people wanted to get away but there was nowhere to run because the police were blocking all the streets and kept on firing. I remember that all Teheran was agitated the following day. You could feel that dark and terrible times were approaching.")

THE DEAD FLAME

The revolution put an end to the Shah's rule. It destroyed the palace and buried the monarchy. It all began with an apparently small mistake on the part of the imperial authority. With that one false step, the monarchy signed its own death warrant.

The causes of a revolution are usually sought in objective conditions—general poverty, oppression, scandalous abuses. But this view, while correct, is one-sided. After all, such conditions exist in a hundred countries, but revolutions erupt rarely. What is needed is the consciousness of poverty and the consciousness of oppression, and the conviction that poverty and oppression are not the natural order of this world. It is curious that in this case, experience in and of itself, no matter how painful, does not suffice. The indispensable catalyst is the word, the explanatory idea. More than petards or stilettoes, therefore, words—uncontrolled words, circulating freely, underground, rebelliously, not gotten up in dress uniforms, uncertified—frighten tyrants. But sometimes it is the official, uniformed, certified words that bring about the revolution.

Revolution must be distinguished from revolt, *coup d'état*, palace takeover. A coup or a palace takeover may be planned, but a revolution—never. Its outbreak, the hour of that outbreak, takes everyone, even those who have been striving for it, unawares. They stand amazed at the spontaneity that appears suddenly and destroys everything in its path. It demolishes so ruthlessly that in the end it may annihilate the ideals that called it into being.

It is a mistaken assumption that nations wronged by history (and they are in the majority) live with the constant thought of revolution, that they see it as the simplest solution. Every revolution is a drama, and humanity instinctively avoids dramatic situations. Even if we find ourselves in such a situation we look feverishly for a way out, we seek calm and, most often, the commonplace. That is why revolutions never last long. They are a last resort, and if people turn to revolution it is only because long experience has taught them there is no other solution. All other attempts, all other means have failed.

Every revolution is preceded by a state of general exhaustion and takes place against a background of unleashed aggressiveness. Authority cannot put up with a nation that gets on its nerves; the nation cannot tolerate an authority it has come to hate. Authority has squandered all its credibility and has empty hands, the nation has lost the final scrap of patience and makes a fist. A climate of tension and increasing oppressiveness prevails. We start to fall into a psychosis of terror. The discharge is coming. We feel it.

As for the technique of the struggle, history knows two types of revolution. The first is revolution by assault, the second revolution by siege. All the future fortune, the success, of a revolution by assault is decided by the reach of the first blow. Strike and seize as much ground as possible! This is important because such a revolution, while the most violent, is also the most superficial. The adversary has been defeated, but in retreating he has preserved a part of his forces. He will counter-attack and force the victor to withdraw. Thus, the more far-reaching the first blow, the greater the area that can be saved in spite of later concessions. In a revolution by assault, the first phase is the most radical. The subsequent phases are a slow but incessant withdrawal to the point at which the two sides, the rebelling and the rebelled-against, reach the final compromise. A revolution by siege is different; here the first strike is usually weak and we can hardly surmise that it forebodes a cataclysm. But events soon gather speed and become dramatic. More and more people take part. The walls behind which authority has been sheltering crack and then burst. The success of a revolution by siege depends on the determination of the rebels, on their will power and endurance. One more day! One more push! In the end, the gates yield, the crowd breaks in and celebrates its triumph.

It is authority that provokes revolution. Certainly, it does not do so consciously. Yet its style of life and way of ruling finally become a provocation. This occurs when a feeling of impunity takes root among the elite: We are allowed anything, we can do anything. This is a delusion, but it rests on a certain rational foundation. For a while it does indeed look as if they can do whatever they want. Scandal after scandal and illegality after illegality go unpunished. The people remain silent, patient, wary. They are afraid and do not yet feel their own strength. At the same time, they keep a detailed account of the wrongs, which at one particular moment are to be added up. The choice of that moment is the greatest riddle known to history. Why did it happen on that day, and not on another? Why did this event, and not some other, bring it about? After all, the government was indulging in even worse excesses only yesterday, and there was no reaction at all. "What have I done?" asks the ruler, at a loss. "What has possessed them all of a sudden?" This is what he has done: He has abused the patience of the people. But where is the limit of that patience? How can it be defined? If the answer can be determined at all, it will be different in each case. The only certain thing is that rulers who know that such a limit exists and know how to respect it can count on holding power for a long time. But there are few such rulers.

How did the Shah violate this limit and pass sentence on himself? Through a newspaper article. Authority ought to know that a careless word can bring down the greatest empire. It seems to know this, seems to be vigilant, and yet at a certain moment the instinct for self-preservation fails and, self-assured and overweening, it commits the mistake of arrogance and perishes. On January 8, 1978, an article attacking Khomeini appeared in the government newspaper *Etelat*. At the time, Khomeini was fighting the Shah from abroad, where he lived as an émigré. Persecuted by the despot, expelled

from the country, Khomeini was the idol and conscience of the people. To destroy the myth of Khomeini
was to destroy something holy, to shatter the hopes of
the wronged and the humiliated. Such exactly was the
intention of the article.

What should one write to ruin an adversary? The best
thing is to prove he is not one of us—the stranger, alien, foreigner. To this end we create the category of the
true family. We here, you and I, the authorities and the
nation, are a true family. We live in unity, among our
own kind. We have the same roof over our heads, we sit
at the same table, we know how to get along with each
other, how to help each other out. Unfortunately, we are
not alone. All around us are hordes of strangers, aliens,
foreigners who want to destroy our peace and quiet and
take over our home. What is a stranger? Above all, a
stranger is someone worse than us—and dangerous at
the same time. If only he were merely worse, and left
well enough alone! Not a chance! He is going to muddy
the waters, make trouble, destroy. He is going to set us
at odds with each other, make fools of us, break us. The
stranger lies in wait for you. He is the cause of your
misfortunes. And where does his power come from?
From the fact that there are strange (foreign, alien) forces
behind him. These forces may be identified or not, but
one thing is certain: They are powerful. Or rather, they
are powerful if we treat them lightly. If, on the other
hand, we remain vigilant and keep fighting, then we will
be stronger. Now look at Khomeini. There's a stranger
for you. His grandfather came from India, so let's ask
ourselves: Whose interest is this foreigner's grandson
serving? That was the first part of the article. The sec-

ond part had to do with health. What a great thing it is that we're healthy! For our true family is also a healthy family. Of sound body and mind. To whom do we owe this health? To our authorities, who have assured us a good, happy life and are therefore the best authorities under the sun. And who could oppose such authorities? Only someone devoid of common sense. Since ours are the best authorities, it would take a madman to fight against them. A sound community must identify such fools and send them away, into isolation. Thus, it's a good thing the Shah expelled him from the country. Otherwise, Khomeini would have had to be locked up in a lunatic asylum.

When this newspaper article reached Qom, it made the people indignant. They congregated in the streets and the squares. Those who could read read aloud to the others. The commotion drew people into larger and larger groups, shouting and debating—interminable debating is a passion with the Iranians, anywhere, at any time of day or night. The groups most agitated by this incessant talk were like magnets; they kept attracting new listeners, until in the end a massive crowd had assembled in the main square. And that is exactly the thing that the police most dislike. Who gave permission for this great mass? Nobody. No permission has been given. And who gave them permission to shout? To wave their hands around? The police know in advance that these were rhetorical questions and that it was time to get down to business.

Now the most important moment, the moment that will determine the fate of the country, the Shah, and the revolution, is the moment when one policeman walks from his post toward one man on the edge of the crowd, raises his voice, and orders the man to go home. The policeman and the man on the edge of the crowd are ordinary, anonymous people, but their meeting has historic significance. They are both adults, they have both lived through certain events, they have both had their individual experiences. The policeman's experience: If I shout at someone and raise my truncheon, he will first go numb with terror and then take to his heels. The experience of the man at the edge of the crowd: At the sight of an approaching policeman I am seized by fear and start running. On the basis of these experiences we can elaborate a scenario: The policeman shouts, the man runs, others take flight, the square empties. But this time everything turns out differently. The policeman shouts, but the man doesn't run. He just stands there, looking at the policeman. It's a cautious look, still tinged with fear, but at the same time tough and insolent. So that's the way it is! The man on the edge of the crowd is looking insolently at uniformed authority. He doesn't budge. He glances around and sees the same look on other faces. Like his, their faces are watchful, still a bit fearful, but already firm and unrelenting. Nobody runs though the policeman has gone on shouting; at last he stops. There is a moment of silence. We don't know whether the policeman and the man on the edge of the crowd already realize what has happened. The man has stopped being afraid—and this is precisely the beginning of the revolution. Here it starts. Until now, whenever these two men approached each other, a third figure instantly inter-

vened between them. That third figure was fear. Fear
was the policeman's ally and the man in the crowd's foe.
Fear interposed its rules and decided everything. Now
the two men find themselves alone, facing each other,
and fear has disappeared into thin air. Until now their
relationship was charged with emotion, a mixture of
aggression, scorn, rage, terror. But now that fear has retreated, this perverse, hateful union has suddenly broken up; something has been extinguished. The two men
have now grown mutually indifferent, useless to each
other; they can go their own ways. Accordingly, the policeman turns around and begins to walk heavily back
toward his post, while the man on the edge of the crowd
stands there looking at his vanishing enemy.

Fear: a predatory, voracious animal living inside us.
It does not let us forget it's there. It keeps eating at us
and twisting our guts. It demands food all the time, and
we see that it gets the choicest delicacies. Its preferred
fare is dismal gossip, bad news, panicky thoughts,
nightmare images. From a thousand pieces of gossip,
portents, ideas, we always cull the worst ones—the ones
that fear likes best. Anything to satisfy the monster and
set it at ease. Here we see a man listening to someone
talking, his face pale and his movements restless. What's
going on? He is feeding his fear. And what if we have
nothing to feed it with? We make something up, feverishly. And what if (seldom though this may occur) we
can't make anything up? We rush to other people, look
for them, ask questions, listen and gather portents, for
as long as it takes to satiate our fear.

All books about all revolutions begin with a chapter that describes the decay of tottering authority or the misery and sufferings of the people. They should begin with a psychological chapter, one that shows how a harassed, terrified man suddenly breaks his terror, stops being afraid. This unusual process, sometimes accomplished in an instant like a shock or a lustration, demands illuminating. Man gets rid of fear and feels free. Without that there would be no revolution.

The policeman returns to his post and reports to the commander. The commander sends in the riflemen and orders them to take up positions on the roofs of the houses around the square. He himself drives to the center of town and uses loudspeakers to call on the crowd to disperse. But no one wants to listen. So he withdraws to a safe place and gives the order to open fire. Automatic-weapons fire cascades onto the heads of the people. Panic breaks out, there is tumult, those who can, escape. Then the shooting stops. The dead remain on the square.

It is not known whether the Shah was shown the pictures of this square photographed by the police after the massacre. Let's say that he was. Let's say that he wasn't. The Shah worked a great deal, and he may not have had time. His working day began at seven in the morning and ended at midnight. He actually rested only in winter, when he went to St. Moritz to ski. Even there he allowed himself only two or three runs before returning to his residence and going back to work. Recalling these occasions, Madame L. states that the Empress behaved very democratically at St. Moritz. As evidence she produces a photograph showing the Empress waiting in line for the ski lift. Yes, just like that—standing there, leaning on her skis, a smart, pleasant woman. And yet, says Madame L., they had so much money that she could have ordered a ski lift built just for herself!

The dead are wrapped in white sheets and laid on wooden biers here. The pallbearers walk briskly, breaking into a trot at times, creating an impression of great haste. The whole procession hurries, there are cries and lamentations, the mourners are restless and uneasy. It is as if the dead man's very presence exasperates them, as if they want to commit him to the earth immediately. Afterwards they lay out food on the grave and the funeral banquet takes place. Whoever passes by is invited to join in and given food. Those who are not hungry get only some fruit, an apple or an orange, but everyone must eat something.

On the following day, the period of commemoration begins. People ponder the dead man's life, his kind heart and upright character. This period lasts forty days. On the fortieth day, family, friends, and acquaintances gather in the home of the deceased. Neighbors collect around the house—the whole street, the whole village, a crowd of people. It is a crowd of commemoration, a lamenting crowd. Pain and grief reach their piercing apogee, their mourning, desperate crescendo. If the death was natural, congruent with the usual human lot, this gathering—which can go on round the clock—consists of some hours of ecstatic, pathetic discharge, followed by a mood of dulled and humble resignation. But if the death was a violent one, inflicted by somebody, a spirit of retaliation and a thirst for revenge seize the people. In an atmosphere of unfettered wrath and aggravated hatred, they pronounce the name of the killer, the author of their sorrow. And it is believed that, even if he is far away, he will shudder at that moment: Yes, his days are numbered.

A nation trampled by despotism, degraded, forced into the role of an object, seeks shelter, seeks a place where it can dig itself in, wall itself off, be itself. This is indispensable if it is to preserve its individuality, its identity, even its ordinariness. But a whole nation cannot emigrate, so it undertakes a migration in time rather than in space. In the face of the encircling afflictions and threats of reality, it goes back to a past that seems a lost paradise. It regains its security in customs so old and therefore so sacred that authority fears to combat them. This is why a gradual rebirth of old customs, beliefs, and symbols occurs under the lid of every dictatorship—in opposition to, against the will of the dictatorship. The old acquires a new sense, a new and provocative meaning. This happens hesitantly and often secretly at first, but as the dictatorship grows increasingly unbearable and oppressive, the strength and scope of the return to the old increase. Some voices call this a regressive return to the middle ages. So it may be. But more often, this is the way the people vent their opposition. Since authority claims to represent progress and modernity, we will show that our values are different. This is more a matter of political spite than a desire to recapture the forgotten world of the ancestors. Only let life get better and the old customs lose their emotional coloration to become again what they were—a ritual form.

Such a ritual, suddenly transformed into a political act under the influence of the growing opposition spirit, was the commemoration of the dead forty days after their death. What had been a ceremony of family and neighbors turned into a protest meeting. Forty days after the Qom events, people gathered in the mosques of many Iranian towns to commemorate the victims of the massacre. In Tabriz, the tension grew so high that an insurrection broke out. A crowd marched through the street shouting "Death to the Shah." The army rolled in and drowned the city in blood. Hundreds were killed, thousands were wounded. After forty days, the towns went into mourning—it was time to commemorate the Tabriz massacre. In one town—Isfahan—a despairing, angry crowd welled into the streets. The army surrounded the demonstrators and opened fire; more people died. Another forty days pass and mourning crowds now assemble in dozens of towns to commemorate those who fell in Isfahan. There are more demonstrations and massacres. Forty days later, the same thing repeats itself in Meshed. Next it happens in Teheran, and then in Teheran again. In the end it is happening in nearly every city and town.

Thus the Iranian revolution develops in a rhythm of explosions succeeding each other at forty-day intervals. Every forty days there is an explosion of despair, anger, blood. Each time the explosion is more horrible—bigger and bigger crowds, more and more victims. The mechanism of terror begins to run in reverse. Terror is used in order to terrify. But now, the terror that the authorities apply serves to excite the nation to new struggles and new assaults.

The Shah's reflex was typical of all despots: Strike first and suppress, then think it over: What next? First display muscle, make a show of strength, and later perhaps demonstrate you also have a brain. Despotic authority attaches great importance to being considered strong, and much less to being admired for its wisdom. Besides, what does wisdom mean to a despot? It means skill in the use of power. The wise despot knows when and how to strike. This continual display of power is necessary because, at root, any dictatorship appeals to the lowest instincts of the governed: fear, aggressiveness toward one's neighbors, bootlicking. Terror most effectively excites such instincts, and fear of strength is the wellspring of terror.

A despot believes that man is an abject creature. Abject people fill his court and populate his environment. A terrorized society will behave like an unthinking, submissive mob for a long time. Feeding it is enough to make it obey. Provided with amusements, it's happy. The rather small arsenal of political tricks has not changed in millennia. Thus, we have all the amateurs in politics, all the ones convinced they would know how to govern if only they had the authority. Yet surprising things can also happen. Here is a well-fed and well-entertained crowd that stops obeying. It begins to demand something more than entertainment. It wants freedom, it demands justice. The despot is stunned. He doesn't know how to see a man in all his fullness and glory. In the end such a man threatens dictatorship, he is its enemy. So it gathers its strength to destroy him.

Although dictatorship despises the people, it takes pains to win their recognition. In spite of being lawless—or rather, because it is lawless—it strives for the appearance of legality. On this point it is exceedingly touchy, morbidly oversensitive. Moreover, it suffers from a feeling (however deeply hidden) of inferiority. So it spares no pains to demonstrate to itself and others the popular approval it enjoys. Even if this support is a mere charade, it feels satisfying. So what if it's only an appearance? The world of dictatorship is full of appearances.

The Shah, too, felt the need of approval. Accordingly, when the last victims of the Tabriz massacre had been buried, a demonstration of support for the monarchy was organized in that city. Activists of the Shah's party, Rastakhiz, were assembled on the great town commons. They carried portraits of their leader with suns painted above his monarchical head. The whole government appeared on the reviewing stand. Prime Minister Jamshid Amuzegar addressed the gathering. The speaker wondered how a few anarchists and nihilists could destroy the nation's unity and upset its tranquility. "They are so few that it is even hard to speak of a group. This is a handful of people." Fortunately, he said, words of condemnation were flowing in from all over the country against those who want to ruin our homes and our well-being—after which a resolution of support for the Shah was passed. When the demonstration ended, the participants sneaked home. Most were carried by buses to the nearby towns from which they'd been imported to Tabriz for the occasion.

After this demonstration, the Shah felt better. He seemed to be getting back on his feet. Until then he had been playing with cards marked with blood. Now he made up his mind to play with a clean deck. To gain popular sympathy, he dismissed a few of the officers who had been in charge of the units that opened fire on the inhabitants of Tabriz. Among the generals, this move caused murmurs of discontent. To appease the generals, he ordered that the inhabitants of Isfahan be fired on. The people responded with an outburst of anger and hatred. He wanted to appease the people, so he dismissed the head of Savak. Savak was appalled. To appease Savak, the Shah allowed them to arrest whomever they wished. And so by reversals, detours, meanderings, and zig-zags, step by step, he drew nearer to the precipice.

The Shah was reproached for being irresolute. Politicians, they say, ought to be resolute. But resolute about what? The Shah was resolute about retaining his throne, and to this end he explored every possibility. He tried shooting and he tried democratizing, he locked people up and he released them, he fired some and promoted others, he threatened and then he commended. All in vain. People simply did not want a Shah anymore; they did not want that kind of authority.

The Shah's vanity did him in. He thought of himself as the father of his country, but the country rose against him. He took it to heart and felt it keenly. At any price (unfortunately, even blood) he wanted to restore the former image, cherished for years, of a happy people prostrate in gratitude before their benefactor. But he forgot that we are living in times when people demand rights, not grace.

He also may have perished because he took himself too literally, too seriously. He certainly believed that the people worshipped him and thought of him as the best and worthiest part of themselves, the highest good. The sight of their revolt was inconceivable, shocking, too much for his nerves. He reckoned he had to react immediately. This led him to violent, hysterical, mad decisions. He lacked a certain dose of cynicism. He could have said: "They're demonstrating? So let them demonstrate. Half a year? A year? I can wait it out. In any case, I won't budge from the palace." And the people, disenchanted and embittered, willy-nilly, would have gone home in the end because it's unreasonable to expect people to spend their whole lives marching in demonstrations. But the Shah didn't want to wait. And in politics you have to know how to wait.

He also perished because he did not know his own country. He spent his whole life in the palace. When he would leave the palace, he would do it like someone sticking his head out the door of a warm room into the freezing cold. Look around a minute and duck back in! Yet the same structure of destructive and deforming laws operates in the life of all palaces. So it has been from time immemorial, so it is and shall be. You can build ten new palaces, but as soon as they are finished they become subject to the same laws that existed in the palaces built five thousand years ago. The only solution is to treat the palace as a temporary abode, the same way you treat a streetcar or a bus. You get on, ride a while, and then get off. And it's very good to remember to get off at the right stop and not ride too far.

The most difficult thing to do while living in a palace is to imagine a different life—for instance, your own life, but outside of and minus the palace. Toward the end, the ruler finds people willing to help him out. Many lives, regrettably, can be lost at such moments. The problem of honor in politics. Take de Gaulle—a man of honor. He lost a referendum, tidied up his desk, and left the palace, never to return. He wanted to govern only under the condition that the majority accept him. The moment the majority refused him their trust, he left. But how many are like him? The others will cry, but they won't move; they'll torment the nation, but they won't budge. Thrown out one door, they sneak in through another; kicked down the stairs, they begin to crawl back up. They will excuse themselves, bow and scrape, lie and simper, provided they can stay—or provided they can return. They will hold out their hands—Look, no blood on them. But the very fact of having to show those hands covers them with the deepest shame. They will turn their pockets inside out—Look, there's not much there. But the very fact of exposing their pockets—how humiliating! The Shah, when he left the palace, was crying. At the airport he was crying again. Later he explained in interviews how much money he had, and that it was less than people thought.

I spent whole days roaming around Teheran with no purpose or end in mind. I was escaping from the wearisome emptiness of my room and from my aggressive, slanderous hag of a cleaning woman. She was always asking for money. She took my clean, pressed shirts when they came back from the laundry, dunked them in water, strung them on a line—and demanded payment. For what? For ruining my shirts? Her scrawny claw was always thrust out from beneath her chador. I knew she had no money. But neither had I. This was something she couldn't understand. A man from the outside world is by definition rich. The hotel owner shrugged her shoulders—"I can't do anything about it. As a result of the revolution, my dear sir, that woman now has power." The hotel owner treated me as a natural ally, a counterrevolutionary. She assumed that my views were liberal; liberals, as people of the center, were at that time under the sharpest attack. Choose between God and Satan! Official propaganda expected a clear declaration from everyone; the time of the purges and of what they called "examining each other's hands" had begun.

I spent December wandering around the city. New Year's Eve, 1979, was approaching. A friend phoned with news that he was planning a party, a genuine, discreetly camouflaged evening of fun, and wanted me to come. I refused, saying I had other plans. What plans? He was astounded, for in fact what could you do in

Teheran on such an evening? Strange plans, I replied, which was as close to the truth as I could come. I'd made up my mind to go to the U.S. Embassy on New Year's Eve. I wanted to see what this place the whole world was talking about would look like that night. I left the hotel at eleven. I didn't have far to walk—a mile and a half, perhaps, easy going because it was downhill. The cold was penetrating, the wind dry and frigid; there must have been a snowstorm raging in the mountains. I walked through streets empty of pedestrians and patrols, empty of everyone but a peanut vendor sitting in his booth in Valiahd Square, all wrapped and muffled against the cold in warm scarves like the autumnal vendors on Polna Street in Warsaw. I bought a bag of peanuts and gave him a handful of rials—too many; it was my Christmas present. He didn't understand. He counted out what I owed him and handed back the change with a serious, dignified expression. Thus was rejected the gesture I'd hoped would bring me at least a momentary closeness with the only other person I'd encountered in the dead, frozen city. I walked on, looking at the decaying shop windows, turned into Takhte-Jamshid, passed a burned-out bank, a fire-scarred cinema, an empty hotel, an unlit airline office. Finally I reached the Embassy. In the daytime, the place is like a big marketplace, a busy encampment, a noisy political amusement park where you come to scream and let off steam. You can come here, abuse the mighty of the world, and not face any consequences at all. There's no lack of volunteers; the place is thronged. But just now, with midnight approaching, there was no one. I walked around what could have been a vast stage long abandoned by the last actors. There remained only pieces of unattended scenery and the disconcerting atmosphere of a ghost town. The wind fluttered the tatters of banners and rippled a big painting of a band of devils warming themselves over the inferno. Further along, Carter in a star-spangled top hat was shaking a bag of gold while the inspired Imam Ali prepared for a martyr's death. A microphone and batteries of speakers still stood on the platform from which excited orators stirred the crowds to wrath and indignation. The sight of those unspeaking loudspeakers deepened the impression of lifelessness, the void. I walked up to the main entrance. As usual, it was closed with a chain and padlock, since no one had repaired the lock in the gate that the crowd broke when it stormed the Embassy. Near the gate, two young guards crouched in the cold as they leaned against the high brick wall, automatic rifles slung over their shoulders—students of the Imam's line. I had the impression they were dozing. In the background, among the trees, stood the lighted building where the hostages were held. But much as I scrutinized the windows, I saw no one, neither figure nor shadow. I looked at my watch. It was midnight, at least in Teheran, and the New Year was beginning. Somewhere in the world clocks were striking, champagne was bubbling, elaborate fêtes were going on amid joy and elation in glittering, colorful halls. That might have been happening on a different planet from this one where there wasn't even the faintest sound or glimmer of light. Standing there freezing, I suddenly began wondering why I had left that other world and come here to this supremely desolate, extremely depressing place. I didn't know. It simply crossed my mind this evening that I ought to be here. I didn't know any of them, those fifty-two Americans and those two Iranians, and I couldn't even communicate with them. Perhaps I had thought something would happen here. But nothing happened.

The anniversary of the Shah's departure and the fall of the monarchy was approaching. To mark the occasion, the television showed dozens of films about the revolution. In many ways they were all alike. The same pictures and situations recurred. Scenes of an enormous procession always made up Act One. It's difficult to convey the dimensions of such a procession. It is a human river, broad and boiling, flowing endlessly, rolling through the main street from dawn till dusk. A flood, a violent flood that in a moment will engulf and drown everything. A forest of upraised, rhythmically menacing fists, portentous forest. A clamoring throng chanting, Death to the Shah! Very few close-ups of faces. The cameramen are fascinated by the sight of this incipient avalanche; they are stricken by the dimensions of what they see, as if they found themselves at the foot of Everest. Over the last months of the revolution these surging millions marched through the streets of every city. They carried no weapons; their strength lay in their numbers and their ardent, unshakeable determination.

Act Two is the most dramatic. The cameramen stand on the roofs of buildings, filming the unfolding scene from above, a bird's-eye view. First they show us what's happening in the street. Two tanks and two armored cars are parked there. Soldiers in helmets and bulletproof vests have already taken up firing positions on the sidewalks and road. They wait. Now the cameramen show the approaching demonstration. First it appears in the distant perspective of the street, but soon we'll see it close up. Yes, there's the head of the procession. Men are marching, and women and children, too. They're wearing white, symbolizing readiness to die. The cameramen show us their faces, still alive. Their eyes. The children, already tired but calm, want to see what's going to happen. The crowd, marching directly toward the tanks, never slowing down or stopping—a hypnotized crowd? spellbound? moonstruck?—marches as if it sees nothing, as if wandering across an uninhabited earth, a crowd that at this moment has already begun to enter heaven. Now the picture trembles because the hands of the cameraman are trembling. A thump, shooting, the whizz of bullets, screams coming from the television. Close-ups of soldiers changing clips. Close-up of a tank turret pivoting from left to right. Close-up of an officer, comic relief, his helmet has fallen over his eyes. Close-up of the pavement, and then the image flies violently up the wall of the house across the street, over the roof and the chimney into blank space with only the edge of a cloud visible, and then an empty frame and blackness. The inscription on the screen says this was the last footage shot by the cameraman, but others survived to retrieve and preserve the testimony.

The last act is the postmortem. The dead are lying here and there, a wounded man is dragging himself toward a gate, ambulances speed past, people are running, a woman is crying, holding out her hands, a thickset, sweaty man is trying to lift someone's body. The crowd has retreated, dispersed, ebbed in chaos, down small side streets. A helicopter skims low over the roofs. The usual traffic has already begun a few blocks away, the everyday life of the city.

I remember one such scene: Demonstrators are marching. As they pass a hospital, they fall silent. The marchers do not want to disturb the patients. Or another sight: Boys trail at the end of the procession, picking up litter and throwing it into trashcans. The road that the demonstrators have walked on must be clean. A fragment of a film: Children are returning home from school. They hear shooting and run toward the bullets, to where soldiers are firing on demonstrators. The children tear sheets from their notebooks and dip them in the fresh blood on the sidewalks and then, holding the bloody pages aloft, run through the streets displaying them to passers-by, as a warning—Watch out! There's shooting over there! The film from Isfahan was shown several times. A demonstration, a sea of heads, is crossing a vast square. Suddenly the army opens fire from all sides. The crowd rushes to escape amid cries, tumult, disorderly flight, and in the end the square empties. Just at the moment when the last survivors flee out of sight, revealing the naked surface of the enormous square, we notice that a legless invalid in a wheelchair has been left at the very center. He too wants to get away, but one wheel is stuck (the film does not show why). He instinctively hides his head between his arms as bullets are flying all around. Then he desperately works the wheels, but instead of moving, he turns around and around in one spot. It's such a shocking spectacle, the soldiers stop firing for a moment, as if awaiting special orders. Silence. We see a broad, empty vista, deep in the center of which, barely perceptible from this distance, looking like a maimed, dying insect, the crooked figure of a solitary human being is still struggling, as the net tightens and closes. They shoot again, with only one target left. Soon motionless for good, he remained (according to the film's narrator) at the center of the square for an hour or two, like a public monument.

The cameramen overuse the long shot. As a result, they lose sight of details. And yet it is through details that everything can be shown. The universe in the raindrop. I miss close-ups of the people who march in the demonstrations. I miss the conversations. That man marching in the demonstration, how full of hopes he is! He is marching because he is counting on something. He is marching because he believes he can get something done. He is sure that he will be better off. He is marching, thinking: So, if we win, nobody's going to treat me like a dog anymore. He's thinking of shoes. He'll buy decent shoes for the whole family. He's thinking of a home. If we win, I'll start living like a human being. A new world: He, an ordinary man, is going to know a minister personally and get everything taken care of. But why a minister! We'll form a committee ourselves to run things! He has other ideas and plans, none too precise or distinct, but they're all good, they're all the kind that cheer you up, because they possess the best of attributes: They'll be carried out. He feels high, he feels the power mounting in him, for as he marches he is also participating, taking his destiny into his hands for the first time, taking part for the first time, exerting influence, deciding about something—he *is*.

I once saw a spontaneous march come about. A man was walking down the street leading to the airport; he was singing. It was a song about Allah—Allah Akbar! He had a fine, carrying voice of splendid, moving tone. He was paying attention to nothing and nobody as he walked. I followed him because I wanted to hear him singing. In a moment a handful of children playing in the street joined him and began to sing. Then there was a group of men and, emerging bashfully from the sides, some women. When there were about a hundred marchers, the crowd began to multiply quickly, at a geometric rate, in fact. A crowd draws a crowd, as Canetti remarked. Here they like to be in a crowd, a crowd strengthens them and adds to their importance. They express themselves through the crowd, they seek the crowd, and in a crowd they obviously get rid of something they carry inside themselves when they are alone, something that makes them feel bad.

On that same street (formerly called Shah Reza and now Engelob) an old Armenian sells spices and dried fruit. Because the inside of the shop is cramped and cluttered, he displays his goods on the sidewalk—bags, baskets, and jars of raisins, almonds, dates, nuts, olives, ginger, pomegranates, plums, pepper, millet, and dozens of other delicacies with names and uses unknown to me. Seen from a distance, against the background of crumbling gray plaster, they look like a rich and colorful palette, like a painting of tasteful and imaginative composition. Moreover, the shopkeeper changes the layout of the colors from day to day: Brown dates lie beside pastel pistachios and green olives—and the next day white almonds have taken the place of the fleshy dates and a pile of pepper pods is burning scarlet where there had been golden millet. Not only for the sake of the sensation do I visit this coloristic design. The daily fate of the exhibition is also a source of information about what's going to happen in politics, for Engelob is the boulevard of demonstrations. If there is no sidewalk display in the morning, then the Armenian is getting ready for a hot day—there will be a demonstration. He would rather hide his fruits and spices than leave them out to be trampled by the crowd. This also means that I have to get down to work and establish who is going to demonstrate, and for what. If, on the other hand, I can see the Armenian's variegated glowing palette from far down Engelob Street, then I know it's going to be an ordinary, peaceful, uneventful day and I can go with easy conscience to Leon's for a glass of whisky.

Further down Engelob Street is a baker's that sells fresh, hot bread. Iranian bread is shaped like a big, flat cake. The oven in which these cakes are baked is a hole dug into the ground, ten feet deep, with walls of inlaid clay. A fire burns at the bottom. If a woman betrays her husband, she is thrown into such a well of fire. Razak Naderi, a boy of twelve, works at this bakery. Somebody ought to make a film about Razak. At the age of nine he came to Teheran looking for work, leaving his mother, two younger sisters, and three younger brothers behind in his village near Zanjan, six hundred miles from the capital. From that time on he has had to support his family. He gets up at four and kneels by the oven door. The fire is roaring, and frightful heat pours out of the oven. With a long rod, Razak sticks the loaves on the clay walls and sees they are taken out when they are done. He works this way until nine in the evening. What he makes, he sends to his mother. His possessions consist of a suitcase and the blanket in which he wraps himself at night. Razak continually changes jobs and is often unemployed. He knows that he can blame only himself. After three or four months he simply begins to long for his mother. He struggles against the feeling for a while, but he ends up getting on the bus and returning to his village. He would like to stay with his mother as long as possible, but he knows he cannot—he is the sole support of the family, and he has to work. He goes back to Teheran and finds that someone else has taken his job. So Razak goes to Gomruk Square, the gathering place of the unemployed. This is the cheap labor market, and whoever comes here sells himself for the lowest wages. Yet Razak has to wait a week or two before someone hires him. He stands on the square all day, freezing, soaked, hungry. Finally a man turns up and notices him. Razak is happy; he is working again. But the joy wears off quickly, the sharp longing soon returns, so he returns again to see his mother and returns again to Gomruk Square. Right next to Razak there is the great world of the Shah, the revolution, Khomeini and the hostages. Everybody is talking about it. Yet Razak's world is even bigger. It is so big that Razak roams around it and can't find a way out.

Engelob Street in autumn and winter, 1978—endless protest demonstrations pass here. The same thing is happening in all the big cities. The revolt is sweeping the country. Strikes begin. Everybody goes on strike; industry and transport stop dead. Despite the tens of thousands of victims, the pressure keeps growing. Yet the Shah stays on the throne, and the palace is not giving in.

In every revolution, a movement grapples with a structure. The movement attacks the structure, trying to destroy it, while the structure defends itself and tries to extinguish the movement. The two forces, equally powerful, have different properties. The properties of a movement are spontaneity, impulsiveness, dynamic expansiveness—and a short life. The properties of a structure are inertia, resilience, and an amazing, almost instinctive ability to survive. A structure is rather easy to create, and incomparably more difficult to destroy. It can long outlast all the reasons that justified its establishment. Many weak or even fictitious states have been called into being. But states, after all, are structures, and none of them will be crossed off the map. There exists a sort of world of structures, all holding one another up. Threaten one and the others, its kindred, rush to its assistance. The elasticity that helps it to survive is another trait of a structure. Backed into a corner, under pressure, it can suck in its belly, contract, and wait for the moment when it can start expanding again. Interestingly, such renewed expansion always takes place exactly where there had been a contraction. Structures tend toward a return to the status quo, which they regard as the best of states, the ideal. This trait belies the inertia of the structure. The structure is capable of reacting only according to the first program fed into it. Enter a new program—nothing happens, it doesn't react. It will wait for the previous program. A structure can also act like a roly-poly toy: Just when it seems to have been knocked over, it pops back up. A movement unaware of this property of the structure will wrestle with it for a long time, then grow weak, and in the end suffer defeat.

The theater of the Shah: The Shah was a director who wanted to create a theater on the highest, international level. He liked the audience, he wanted to please. Yet he never knew the true nature of art, never had the imagination and wisdom a director needs, and thought that money and a title were enough. He created an enormous stage on which action could unfold in many places simultaneously. On that stage he decided to mount a play titled *The Great Civilization*. He imported scenery from abroad for vast sums. There were all sorts of devices, machines, equipment—whole mountains of concrete, cable, and plastic. Many of the props were actual armaments: tanks, planes, rockets. Elated, proud, the Shah strutted across the stage, listening to the paeans and speeches of approval that flowed from a multitude of loudspeakers. The spotlights played across the scenery, and then converged on the figure of the Shah. He stood or walked in their beams. It was a one-character play, and the actor was also the director. Everyone else was an extra. Generals, ministers, distinguished ladies, lackeys—the great court—moved across the upper level of the stage. Below came the intermediate levels, and at the very bottom the extras of the lowest category. These were the most numerous. Enticed by high wages—the Shah had promised them mountains of gold—they flocked into the cities from the poor villages. The Shah was always on stage, monitoring the action and directing the extras. If he made a gesture, the generals would stand at attention, the ministers would kiss his hand, and the ladies would curtsey. When he walked down to one of the lower levels and nodded his head, officials would rush to his presence in the expectation of prizes and promotions. Only rarely and briefly would he appear on the ground floor of the stage. The extras there behaved apathetically. They were lost, oppressed by the city, uncertain of themselves, cheated and exploited. They felt like foreigners amid the unfamiliar scenery, in the hostile aggressive world surrounding them. The only point of reference in the alien landscape was the mosque, for there had also been a mosque in the village. So they went to the mosque.

The play takes place on several levels at the same time; many things are happening on stage. The scenery begins to move and light up, wheels turn, chimneys smoke, tanks roll back and forth, ministers kiss the Shah, officials hurry after rewards, policemen frown, mullahs talk and talk, extras keep their mouths shut and work. There is more and more crowding and bustle. The Shah walks, beckoning here and pointing a finger there, always in the spotlight. Suddenly confusion breaks out on stage as if everyone had forgotten his part. Yes, they're throwing away the script and making up lines on their own. Revolt in the theater! The spectacle turns into something else, it becomes a violent, rapacious spectacle. The extras from the ground floor, long disenchanted, ill-paid, despised, begin storming the upper levels. Those on the intermediate levels now become rebellious as well and join the ones from the bottom. The black flags of the Shiites appear on stage and the war song of the demonstrators pours from the loudspeakers. Allah Akbar! Tanks roll back and forth, the police open fire. The prolonged cry of the muezzin resounds from the minaret. On the highest level, there is unprecedented confusion. Ministers stuff bags full of banknotes and take flight, ladies grab jewelry boxes and vanish, butlers wander around as though lost. Green-jacketed fedayeens and mujahedeens appear, armed to the teeth. They've taken over the arsenals. The soldiers who used to fire on the crowds now fraternize with the people and stick red carnations in the barrels of their rifles. Candy is strewn over the stage; in the universal joy, shopkeepers are throwing basketsful of sweets to the crowds. Even though it is noon, all the cars have their headlights on. A big assembly is taking place in the cemetery. Everybody is there, weeping for those killed. A mother says that her son, a soldier, committed suicide rather than fire on his brethren, the demonstrators. The gray-haired Ayatollah Teleghani makes a speech. One by one, the spotlights go out. In the last scene the gem-encrusted peacock throne—the throne of the Shahs—comes down from the top floor to the ground floor in dazzling, many-colored radiance. On the throne sits an extraordinary, outsized figure of majestic sublimity, radiating a stunning brilliance of its own. Its hands and feet, its head and its body, are connected to wires and cables. The sight of this figure overpowers us, we dread it, we feel a reflex that would bring us to our knees. But a group of electricians comes on stage, unplugging the cables and cutting the wires. The brilliance begins to fade, and the figure itself grows smaller and more ordinary. Finally the electricians step aside and an elderly, slim man, indeed the kind of gentleman we might encounter at a movie, in a café, or in a line, rises from the throne, brushes his suit, straightens his tie, and walks off stage on his way to the airport.

The picture was clipped from a newspaper so carelessly the caption is missing. It shows a monument of a man on a horse, atop a tall granite pedestal. The rider, a figure of herculean build, is seated comfortably in the saddle, his left hand resting on its horn, his right pointing to something ahead (probably the future). A rope is tied around the neck of the rider, and a similar rope around that of his mount. In the square at the base of the monument stand groups of men pulling on the two lines. All this is taking place in a thronged plaza, with the crowd watching as the men tugging on the ropes strain against the resistance of the massive bronze statue. The photograph captures the very moment when the ropes are stretched tight as piano wires and the rider and his mount are just tilting to the side—an instant before they crash to earth. We can't help wondering if these men pulling ropes with so much effort and self-denial will be able to jump out of the way, especially since the gawkers crowded into the plaza have left them little room. This photograph shows the pulling down of a monument to one of the Shahs (father or son) in Teheran or some other Iranian city. It is hard to be sure about the year the photograph was taken, since the monuments of both Pahlavis were pulled down several times, whenever the occasion presented itself to the people.

A reporter from the Teheran newspaper *Kayhan* interviewed a man who wrecks monuments to the Shah:
—You've won a certain popularity in your neighborhood, Golam, as a man who pulls down monuments. You're even regarded as a sort of veteran in the field.

—That's right. I first pulled down monuments in the time of the old Shah, that is the father of Mohammed Reza, when he abdicated in '41. I remember what great joy there was in the city when news got around the old Shah had stepped down. Everybody rushed out to smash his monuments. I was just a young boy then, but I helped my father and the neighbors pull down the monument that Reza Khan had set up to himself in our neighborhood. I could say that that was my baptism of fire.

—Were you persecuted for it?

—Not on that occasion.

—Do you remember '53?

—Of course I remember. Wasn't that the most important year, when democracy ended and the regime began? In any case, I recall the radio saying that the Shah had escaped to Europe. When the people heard that, they went out into the street and started pulling down the monuments. And I have to say that the young Shah had been putting up monuments to himself and his father from the beginning, so over the years a lot accumulated that needed pulling down. My father was no longer alive then, but I was grown up and for the first time I brought them down on my own.

—So did you destroy all his monuments?

—Yes, every last one. By the time the Shah came back, there wasn't a Pahlavi monument left. But he started right back in, putting up monuments to himself and his father.

—Does that mean that you would pull down, he would set up, then you would pull down what he had set up, and it kept going on like this?

—That's right. Many times we nearly threw in the towel. If we pulled one down, he set up three. If we pulled down three, he set up ten. There was no end in sight.

—And when was the next time, after '53, that you wrecked them again?

—We intended to go to work in '63, when the rebellion broke out after the Shah imprisoned Khomeini. But instead the Shah began such a massacre that, far from pulling down monuments, we had to hide our hawsers.

—Am I to understand you had special hawsers for the job?

—Yes indeed! We hid our stout sisal rope with a rope-seller at the bazaar. It was no joke. If the police had picked up our trail, we would have gone to the wall. We had everything prepared for the right moment, all thought out and practiced. During the last revolution, I mean in '79, all those disasters happened because a lot of amateurs were knocking down monuments, and there were accidents when they pulled the statues onto their own heads. It's not easy to pull down monuments. It takes experience, expertise. You have to know what they're made of, how much they weigh, how high they are, whether they're welded together or sunk in cement, where to hook the line on, which way to pull, and how to smash them once they're down. We were already working at pulling it down each time they set up a new monument to the Shah. That was the best chance to get a good look and see how it was built, whether the figure was hollow or solid, and, most important, how it was attached to the pedestal and how it was reinforced.

—It must have taken up a lot of your time.

—Right! More and more monuments were going up in the last few years. Everywhere—in the squares, in the streets, in the stations, by the road. And besides, there were others setting up monuments as well. Whoever

wanted to get a jump on the competition for a good contract hurried to be the first one to put up a monument.
That's why a lot of them were built cheaply and, when
the time came, they were easy to bring down. But, I have
to admit, there were times when I doubted we'd get them
all. There were hundreds of them. But we weren't afraid
to work up a sweat. My hands were all blisters from the
ropes.

—So, Golam, you've had an interesting line of work.

—It wasn't work. It was duty. I'm very proud to have
been a wrecker of the Shah's monuments. I think that
everyone who took part is proud to have done so. What
we did is plain for all to see. All the pedestals are empty,
and the figures of the Shahs have either been smashed
or are lying in backyards somewhere.

The Shah had created a system capable only of de-
fending itself, but incapable of satisfying the people. This
was its greatest weakness and the true cause of its ultimate defeat. The psychological foundation of such a
system is the ruler's scorn for his people and his conviction that the ignorant nation can always be deceived by
continual promises. But there is an Iranian proverb that
says: Promises have value only for those who believe in
them.

Khomeini returned from exile and stayed briefly in
Teheran before leaving for Qom. Everyone wanted to see
him, several million people were waiting to shake his
hand. Crowds besieged the school building where he was
staying. Everyone felt entitled to a meeting with the ayatollah. After all, they had fought for his return. They

had shed their blood. Elation and euphoria were in the air. People walked around slapping each other on the back, as if to say to each other—See! We can do anything!

Seldom does a people live through such moments! But just then the sense of victory seemed natural and justified. The Shah's Great Civilization lay in ruins. What had it been in essence? A rejected transplant. It had been an attempt to impose a certain model of life on a community attached to entirely different traditions and values. It was forced, an operation that had more to do with surgical success in itself than with the question of whether the patient remained alive or—equally important—remained himself.

The rejection of a transplant—once it begins, the process is irreversible. All it takes is for society to accept the conviction that the imposed form of existence does more harm than good. Soon the discontent becomes manifest, at first covertly and passively, then more and more overtly and assertively. There will be no peace until the imposed, alien body is purged. The organism grows deaf to persuasion and argument. It remains feverish, unable to reflect. And yet there were noble intentions and lofty ideals behind the Great Civilization. But the people saw them only as caricatures, that is, in the guise that ideals are given when translated into practice. In this way even sublime ideals become subject to doubt.

And afterward? What happened afterward? What should I write about now? About the way that a great experience comes to an end? A melancholy topic, for a revolt is a great experience, an adventure of the heart. Look at the people who are taking part in a revolt. They are stimulated, excited, ready to make sacrifices. At that moment they are living in a monothematic world limited to one thought: to attain the goal they are fighting for. Everything will be subjugated to that goal; every inconvenience becomes bearable; no sacrifice is too great. A revolt frees us from our own ego, from that everyday ego that now strikes us as small, nondescript—alien. Astounded, we discover in ourselves unknown energies and are capable of such noble behavior that we ourselves look on with admiration. And how much pride we feel at being able to rise so high! What satisfaction at being able to give so much of ourselves! But there comes a moment when the mood burns out and everything ends. As a matter of reflex, out of custom, we go on repeating the gestures and the words and want everything to be the way it was yesterday, but we know already—and the discovery appalls us—that this yesterday will never again return. We look around and make another discovery: those who were with us have also changed—something has burned out in them, as well, something has been extinguished. Our community falls suddenly to pieces and everyone returns to his everyday I, which pinches at first like ill-fitting shoes—but we know that they are our shoes and we are not going to get any others. We look uncomfortably into each other's eyes, we shy away from conversation, we stop being any use to one another.

This fall in temperature, this change of climate, belongs among the most unsettling and depressing of experiences. A day begins in which something should happen. And nothing happens. Nobody comes to call, nobody is waiting for us, we are superfluous. We begin to feel a great fatigue, apathy gradually engulfs us. We tell ourselves: I have to rest up, get in shape, build up my strength. We have to get some fresh air. We have to do something mundane—straighten up the apartment, fix the window. These are all defensive actions aimed at dodging the imminent depression. So we pull ourselves together and fix the window. But everything is not in order, we are not joyful, because the pebble stuck inside us keeps nagging.

I too shared that feeling that comes over us when we sit before a dying fire. I walked around a Teheran from which the traces of yesterday's experiences were vanishing. They were vanishing suddenly, and you could get the impression that nothing had happened here. A few burned cinemas, a few demolished banks—the symbols of foreign influence. Revolution attaches great importance to symbols, destroying some monuments and setting up others to replace them in the hope that through metaphor it can survive. And what of the people? Once again they had become pedestrian citizens, going somewhere, standing around street fires warming their hands, part of the dull landscape of a grey town. Once again each was alone, each for himself, closed and taciturn. Could they still have been waiting for something to happen, for some extraordinary event? I don't know, I can't say.

Everything that makes up the outward, visible part of a revolution vanishes quickly. A person, an individual being, has a thousand ways of conveying his feelings and thoughts. He is riches without end, he is a world in which we can always discover something new. A crowd, on the other hand, reduces the individuality of the person; a man in a crowd limits himself to a few forms of elementary behavior. The forms through which a crowd can express its yearnings are extraordinarily meager and continually repeat themselves: the demonstration, the strike, the rally, the barricades. That is why you can write a novel about a man, but about a crowd—never. If the crowd disperses, goes home, does not reassemble, we say that the revolution is over.

Now I visited the committee headquarters. Committees—that's what they called the organs of the new power. Unshaven men were sitting around tables in cramped, littered rooms. For the first time, I saw their faces. On my way here I had filed in my memory the names of people who had actively opposed the Shah or supported the rebels from the sidelines. Just such people, I assumed logically, ought to be running things now. I asked where I could find them. The members of the committee did not know. In any case, they weren't here. The whole durable structure in which one man held power, a second opposed him, a third made money, and a fourth criticized, the whole complex setup that had lasted for years, had been blown away like a house of cards. The names I asked about meant nothing to these bearded, barely literate oafs. What did they care that a couple of years ago Hafez Farman had criticized the Shah and paid for it with his job, while Kulsum Kitab was kissing ass and making a career for himself? That was the past. That world no longer existed. The revolution had transferred power to utterly new, anonymous people no one had heard of only yesterday. Now the bearded ones sat and deliberated full time. About what? About what was to be done. Yes, because the committee should do something. One after the other, they spoke. Each wanted to have his say, to make his speech. Watching, you could feel that this was essential to them, that they attached great weight to it. Each of them could go home afterward and tell his neighbors, I made a speech. People could ask each other, Did you hear about his speech? When he walked down the street, they could button-hole him to say respectfully, You made an interesting speech! An informal hierarchy gradually shaped itself: At the top stood those who inevitably made impressive public appearances, while the bottom consisted of intro-verts, people with speech defects, whole hosts of those who could not overcome their stagefright, and finally those who could not see the point of endless blabbing. The next day the talkers would start from scratch, as though nothing had happend the day before, as if they had to begin all over again.

Iran—it was the twenty-seventh revolution I have seen in the Third World. Amid the smoke and the roar, rul-ers would change, governments fall, new people take their seat. But one thing was invariable, indestructible, and—I dread saying it—eternal: the helplessness. These chambers of the Iranian committees reminded me of what I had seen in Bolivia, Mozambique, the Sudan, Benin. What should we do? Do you know what to do? Me? Not me. Maybe you know. Are you talking to me? I'd go whole hog. But how? How do you go whole hog? Ah, yes, that's the problem. Everyone agrees: That is indeed a problem worth discussing. Cigarette smoke clouds the stuffy rooms. There are some good speeches, some not-so-good, a few downright brilliant. After a truly good speech, everyone feels satisfied; they have taken part in something that was a genuine success.

The whole thing began to intrigue me, so I sat down in one of the committee headquarters (pretending to wait for someone who was not there) and watched how they settled the simplest of problems. After all, life consists of settling problems, progress of settling them deftly and to the general satisfaction. After a while a woman came in to ask for a certificate. The man who could issue it was tied up in a discussion at the moment. The woman waited. People here have a fantastic talent for waiting— they can turn to stone and remain motionless forever. Eventually the man turned up, and they began talking. The woman spoke, he asked a question, the woman asked a question, he said something. After some haggling, they agreed. They began looking for a piece of paper. Various pieces of paper lay on the table, but none of them looked right. The man disappeared—he must have gone to look for paper, but he might just as well have gone across the street to drink some tea (it was a hot day). The woman waited in silence. The man returned, wiping his mouth in satisfaction (so he'd gone for tea after all), but he also had paper. Now began the most dramatic part of all—the search for a pencil. Nowhere was there a pencil, not on the table, nor in the drawer, nor on the floor. I lent him my pen. He smiled, and the woman sighed with relief. Then he sat down to write. As he began writing, he realized he was not quite sure what he was supposed to be certifying. They began talking, and the man nodded. Finally, the document was ready. Now it had to be signed by someone higher up. But the higher-up was unavailable. He was debating in another committee, and there was no way to get in touch with him because the telephone was not answering. Wait. The woman turned back into stone, the man disappeared, and I left to have some tea.

Later, that man will learn how to write certificates and will know how to do many other things. But after a few years, there will be another upheaval, the man we already know will be gone, and his place will fall to someone new who will start fumbling around for a piece of paper and a pencil. The same woman or another one will turn herself to stone and wait. Somebody will lend his pen. The higher-up will be busy debating. All of them, like their predecessors, will begin to move in the spellbound circle of helplessness. Who created that circle? In Iran, it was the Shah. The Shah thought that urbanization and industrialization are the keys to modernity, but this is a mistaken idea. The key to modernity is the village. The Shah got drunk on visions of atomic power plants, computerized production lines, and large-scale petrochemical complexes. But in an underdeveloped country, these are mere mirages of modernity. In that kind of country, most of the people live in poor villages from which they flee to the city. They form a young, energetic workforce that knows little (they are often illiterate) but possesses great ambition and is ready to fight for everything. In the city they find an entrenched establishment linked in one way or another with the prevailing authorities. So they first learn the ropes, settle in a bit, occupy starting positions, and go on the attack. In the struggle they make use of whatever ideology they have brought from the village—usually this is religion. Since they are the ones who are truly determined to get ahead, they often succeed. Then authority passes into their hands. But what are they to do with it? They begin to debate, and they enter the spellbound circle of helplessness. The nation stays alive somehow, as it must, and in the meantime they live better and better. For a while they are satisfied. Their successors are now roaming the vast plains, grazing camels, tending sheep, but they too will grow up, move to the city, and start struggling. What is the rule in all of this? That the newcomers invariably have more ambition than skill. As a result, with each upheaval, the country goes back to the starting point because the victorious new generation has to learn all over again what it cost the defeated generation so much toil to master. And does this mean that the defeated ones were efficient and wise? Not at all—the preceding generation sprang from the same roots as those who took its place. How can the spellbound circle of helplessness be broken? Only by developing the villages. As long as the villages are backward, the country will be backward—even if it contains five thousand factories. As long as the son who has moved to the city visits his native village a few years later as if it were some exotic land, the nation to which he belongs will never be modern.

When the committees discussed what to do next, everyone agreed on one point: Revenge came first. So the executions began. They found some sort of satisfaction in this activity. The newspapers carried front-page photographs of blindfolded people and the boys who were taking aim at them. The papers described these events at length and in detail. What the condemned said before death, how he behaved, what he wrote in his last letter. These executions evoked great indignation in Europe, but few people here understood such complaints. For them the principle of revenge was older than history. A Shah ruled, and then he was beheaded; a new one came along and he was beheaded. How else could you get rid of a Shah? He's not going to resign on his own, is he? Leave him and his supporters alive? The first thing you know, he'll organize an army and make a comeback. Put them in prison? They'll bribe the guards, make an escape, and start massacring whoever toppled them. In such a situation, killing is some sort of elementary reflex of self-preservation. This is a world in which the law is not understood as an instrument to protect man, but as a tool to destroy the adversary. Yes, it sounds cruel; there is a ghastly, implacable ruthlessness about it. Ayatollah Khalkali told us, a group of journalists, that after passing a sentence of death on former Prime Minister Hoveyda he suddenly became suspicious of the firing squad that was to carry out the sentence. He was afraid that they might let Hoveyda get away. So he took Hoveyda into his car. It was night, and, according to Khalkali, they sat talking in the car. About what, he did not say. Wasn't he afraid the condemned man would escape? No, no such thought occurred to him. Time passed. Khalkali was trying to think of someone he could entrust Hoveyda to. Finally he remembered some members of a particular committee near the bazaar. He took Hoveyda to them and left him there.

I am trying to understand them, but over and over again I stumble into a dark region and lose my way. They have a different attitude to life and death. They react differently to the sight of blood. At the sight of blood they become tense, fascinated, they fall into some sort of mystical trance; I can see their animated gestures and hear their cries. The owner of a nearby restaurant pulled up in front of my hotel in his new car. It was a brand-new Pontiac, gold, straight from the dealer. There was some commotion and I could hear chickens being slaughtered in the courtyard. First the people sprinkled the chicken blood over themselves, and then they smeared it on the body of the car. In a moment the automobile was red and dripping blood. This was the baptism of the Pontiac. Wherever there is blood, they crowd around to dip their hands in it. They could not explain to me why this is necessary.

For a few hours a week they manage to attain fantastic discipline. This happens on Friday, at the time of common prayer. That morning the first, most fervent Muslim walks into the vast square, spreads his rug, and kneels on its fringe. Then the next one comes and spreads his rug beside the first one's, even though the whole rest of the square is empty. Then comes the next believer, and the next. Later there are a thousand more, and then a million. They spread their rugs and kneel. They kneel in even, orderly rows, in silence, facing Mecca. Around noon the leader of the Friday prayer begins the ritual. They all stand, bow seven times, straighten up, squat on their haunches, fall to their knees, prostrate themselves, sit on their heels, and prostrate themselves once again. The perfect, undisturbed rhythm of a million bodies is a sight difficult to describe and—for me—rather an ominous one. When the prayers end, fortunately, the ranks break up at once, everyone starts gabbing, and pleasant, free-and-easy confusion dispels the tension.

Dissent soon broke out in the revolutionary camp. Everyone had opposed the Shah and wanted to remove him, but everyone had imagined the future differently. Some thought that the country would become the sort of democracy they knew from their stays in France and Switzerland. But these were exactly the people who lost first in the battle that began once the Shah was gone. They were intelligent people, even wise, but weak. They found themselves at once in a paradoxical situation: A democracy cannot be imposed by force, the majority must favor it, yet the majority wanted what Khomeini wanted—an Islamic republic. When the liberals were gone, the proponents of the republic remained. But they began fighting among themselves as well. In this struggle the conservative hardliners gradually gained the upper hand over the enlightened and open ones. I knew people from both camps, and whenever I thought about the people I sympathized with, pessimism swept over me. The leader of the enlightened ones was Bani Sadr. Slim, slightly stooping, always wearing a polo shirt, he would walk around, persuade, constantly enter into discussions. He had a thousand ideas, he talked a lot—too much—he dreamed incessantly of new solutions, he wrote books in a difficult, obscure style. In these countries an intellectual in politics is always out of place. An intellectual has too much imagination, he tends to hesitate, he is liable to go off in all directions at once. What good is a leader who does not know himself what he ought to stand up for? Beheshti, the hardliner, never behaved in this way. He would summon his staff and dictate instructions, and they were all grateful to him because now they knew how to act and what to do. Beheshti held the reins of the Shiite leadership, Bani Sadr commanded his friends and followers. Bani Sadr's power base lay among the intelligentsia, the students, and the mujahedeen. Beheshti's base was a crowd waiting for the call of the mullahs. It was clear that Bani Sadr had to lose. But Beheshti too would fall before the hand of the Charitable and Merciful One.

Combat squads appeared on the streets. These were groups of strong young people with knives sticking out of their hip pockets. They attacked students, and ambulances carried injured girls out of the university. Demonstrations began, the crowds shook their fists. But against whom this time? Against the man who wrote books in a difficult, obscure style. Millions of people were out of work, the peasants were still living in miserable mud huts, but what did that matter? Beheshti's men were engaged elsewhere—fighting the counterrevolution. Yes, they knew at last what to do and what to say. You don't have anything to eat? You have nowhere to live? We will show you who is to blame. It's that counterrevolutionary. Destroy him, and you can start living like a human being. But what sort of a counterrevolutionary is he—weren't we fighting together only yesterday against the Shah? That was yesterday, and today he's your enemy. Having heard this, the feverish crowd attacked without pausing to think whether the enemy was a real enemy, but you can't blame the people in the crowd. They want a better life and have wanted it for a long time without knowing, without understanding how it is that, despite continuous effort, sacrifice, and self-denial, that better life is still beyond the horizon.

Depression reigned among my friends. They predicted an imminent cataclysm. As always when hard times are coming, they, the intelligent ones, were losing their strength and their faith. They were filled with fear and frustration. They, who once would not have missed a demonstration for anything, now began to fear crowds. As I talked with them, I thought of the Shah. The Shah was traveling around the world and his face would appear in the papers occasionally, each time more wasted. Until the end he thought he would return to his country. He never did, but much of what he had done remained. A despot may go away, but no dictatorship comes to a complete end with his departure. A dictatorship depends for its existence on the ignorance of the mob; that's why all dictators take such pains to cultivate that ignorance. It requires generations to change such a state of affairs, to let some light in. Before this can happen, however, those who have brought down a dictator often act, in spite of themselves, like his heirs, perpetuating the attitudes and thought patterns of the epoch they themselves have destroyed. This happens so involuntarily and subconsciously that they burst into righteous ire if anyone points it out to them. But can all this be blamed on the Shah? The Shah inherited an existing tradition, he moved within the bounds of a set of customs that had prevailed for centuries. It is one of the most difficult things in the world to cross such boundaries, to change the past.

When I want to cheer myself up, I head for Ferdousi Street, where Mr. Ferdousi sells Persian carpets. Mr. Ferdousi, who has passed all his life in the familiar intercourse of art and beauty, looks upon the surrounding reality as if it were a B-film in a cheap, unswept cinema. It is all a question of taste, he tells me: The most important thing, sir, is to have taste. The world would look far different if a few more people had a drop more taste. In all horrors (for he does call them horrors), like lying, treachery, theft, and informing, he distinguishes a common denominator—such things are done by people with no taste. He believes that the nation will survive everything and that beauty is indestructible. You must remember, he tells me as he unfolds another carpet (he knows I am not going to buy it, but he would like me to enjoy the sight of it), that what has made it possible for the Persians to remain themselves over two and a half millennia, what has made it possible for us to remain ourselves in spite of so many wars, invasions, and occupations, is our spiritual, not our material, strength—our poetry, and not our technology; our religion, and not our factories. What have we given the world? We have given poetry, the miniature, and carpets. As you can see, these are all useless things from the productive viewpoint. But it is through such things that we have expressed our true selves. We have given the world this miraculous, unique uselessness. What we have given the world has not made life any easier, only adorned it—if such a distinction makes any sense. To us a carpet, for example, is a vital necessity. You spread a carpet on a wretched, parched desert, lie down on it, and feel you are lying in a green meadow. Yes, our carpets remind us of meadows in flower. You see before you flowers, you see a garden, a pool, a fountain. Peacocks are sauntering among the shrubs. And carpets are things that last—a good carpet will retain its color for centuries. In this way, living in a bare, monotonous desert, you seem to be living in an eternal garden from which neither color nor freshness ever fades. Then you can continue imagining the fragrance of the garden, you can listen to the murmur of the stream and the song of the birds. And then you feel whole, you feel eminent, you are near paradise, you are a poet.

TRAVELS WITH HERODOTUS

In the 1950s, Ryszard Kapuściński finished university in Poland and became a foreign correspondent, hoping to go abroad—perhaps to Czechoslovakia. Instead, he was sent to India—the first stop on a decades-long tour of the world that took him from Iran to El Salvador, from Angola to Armenia. Revisiting his memories of traveling the globe with a copy of Herodotus's *Histories* in tow, Kapuściński describes his awakening to the intricacies and idiosyncrasies of new environments and how the words of the Greek historiographer helped shape his own view of an increasingly globalized world. Written with supreme eloquence and a constant eye to the global undercurrents that have shaped the last half-century, *Travels with Herodotus* is an exceptional chronicle of one man's journey across continents.

Memoir/History

ANOTHER DAY OF LIFE

In 1975, Angola was tumbling into pandemonium; everyone was desperate to abandon the beleaguered colony. A promised land for generations of poor Portuguese, Angola had belonged to Portugal since before there were English speakers in North America. After the collapse of the fascist dictatorship in Portugal in 1974, Angola was brusquely cut loose, spurring the catastrophe of a civil war. Ryszard Kapuściński plunged right into the middle of the drama, recording his impressions of the young soldiers—from Cuba, Angola, South Africa, Portugal—fighting a nebulous war with global repercussions, and examining the peculiar brutality of a country surprised and divided by its newfound freedom.

History

In 1957, Ryszard Kapuściński arrived in Africa to witness the beginning of the end of colonial rule as the first African correspondent of Poland's state newspaper. From the early days of independence in Ghana to the ongoing ethnic genocide in Rwanda, Kapuściński crisscrossed vast distances pursuing the swift and often violent events that followed liberation. Kapuściński hitchhikes with caravans, wanders the Sahara with nomads, and lives in the poverty-stricken slums of Nigeria. What emerges is an extraordinary depiction of Africa—not as a group of nations or geographic locations—but as a vibrant and frequently joyous montage of peoples, cultures, and encounters. Kapuściński's trenchant observations, wry analysis, and overwhelming humanity paint a remarkable portrait of the continent and its people. His unorthodox approach and profound respect for the people he meets challenge conventional understandings of the modern problems faced by Africa at the dawn of the twenty-first century.

History

IMPERIUM

Imperium begins with Ryszard Kapuściński's account of the Soviet occupation of his town in eastern Poland in 1939. It culminates fifty years later, with a forty-thousand-mile journey that takes him from the haunted corridors of the Kremlin to the abandoned gulag of Kolyma, from a miners' strike in the Arctic Circle to a panic-stricken bus ride through the war-torn Caucasus. Out of passivity and paranoia, ethnic hatred and religious fanaticism that have riven two generations of Eastern Europeans, Kapuściński has composed a symphony for a collapsing empire—a work that translates history into the hopes and sufferings of the human beings condemned to live it.

History

THE SOCCER WAR

Part diary and part reportage, *The Soccer War* is a remarkable chronicle of war in the late twentieth century. Between 1958 and 1980, Kapuściński covered twenty-seven revolutions and coups in Africa, Latin America, and the Middle East. Here, with characteristic cogency and emotional immediacy, he recounts the stories behind his official press dispatches—searing firsthand accounts of the frightening, grotesque, and comically absurd aspects of life during war. *The Soccer War* is a singular work of journalism.

History

THE EMPEROR
Downfall of an Autocrat

His Imperial Majesty the Conquering Lion of the Tribe of Judah, Haile Selassie I, King of Kings, Elect of God, Emperor of Ethiopia, reigned from 1930 until he was overthrown by the army in 1974. While the fighting still raged, Ryszard Kapuściński, Poland's leading foreign correspondent, traveled to Ethiopia to seek out and interview Selassie's servants and closest associates on how the emperor had ruled and why he fell. This is Kapuściński's rendition of their accounts—humorous, frightening, grotesque—of a man living amid nearly unimaginable pomp and luxury while his people teetered between hunger and starvation.

History

Printed in the United States
by Baker & Taylor Publisher Services